The
Neurotic
Trillionaire

1 000 000

A SURVEY OF MR. NIXON'S AMERICA

$$000\ 000$$

THE NEUROTIC TRILLIONAIRE

NORMAN MACRAE

Deputy Editor of *The Economist*

HARCOURT BRACE JOVANOVICH, INC.

New York

Foreword

It is not often one can find a short book that encompasses
so many qualities. We have here a detached overview of
the recent history of our economy that could only have been
furnished by a visitor from another land. Written with in-
cisiveness and urbanity, this survey exhibits an understanding not only of the events themselves but, in addition, of
the relevant economic principles. It can serve as a brief
economic history, as a description of the problems in political economy that face the federal, state, and local governments of our country, and as a case study in the strengths
and limitations of Keynesian analysis in action.

The reader is offered a clear description of the vicissitudes
of fiscal and monetary policy in recent years. Beginning
with the relatively slow growth of gross national product
that faced the newly inaugurated Kennedy administration,
the author goes on to describe the implementation of various measures prescribed by the "new economics" to stimulate the rate of economic expansion. The astonishing suc-
cess of these measures at the beginning of the Johnson
administration is brought out to the reader along with the
inflationary problems that soon began to plague it. The limitations of these policies where fine tuning is called for—their

inability to deal with mild unemployment without stimulating price and wage increases—come through very clearly. Along with this there emerges a lesson that many of us have begun to learn a little late: that rapid growth and continued prosperity also exact their social cost. The increasing seriousness of the consequences, especially for the environment and transportation, and the general effects that threaten the quality of life are seen at least in part as unexpected companions to a high level of private income. Finally, the author turns to the problems of the cities and the social upheavals that emerge from them.

In sum, the reader has before him a coherent overview of the triumphs and the frustrations of the designers of economic policy. It makes clear the nature of the vital problems that remain to be solved. Finally, it serves as a body of illustrative material that can bring to the student the significance of the macroeconomic analysis that might otherwise remain a remote body of abstractions.

WILLIAM J. BAUMOL
Princeton University
January 9, 1970

Preface

I visited the United States to collect material for this survey in February and March of 1969. It was published as a special supplement to *The Economist*—the London weekly newspaper for which I work—on May 10, 1969. The text will show fairly clearly whom I interviewed in America, what I was trying to find out, and what my conclusions were.

As the survey is reprinted in America, I have been asked to say in this preface which conclusions I still stick to, and which I would like to trim. How far should the judgments set down be modified by a year's experience of the Nixon administration in action (or, some cruel people would say, in inaction)?

One role seems to me to have been performed rather well. I think that the Nixon administration really has given some sort of sedative to the neurotic trillionaire, and probably more effectively than any alternative administration could have done. Seen from a distance of 3,500 miles, it seems clear that Mr Nixon's main aim during 1969 has been to row America out of the Vietnam war. I use the word "row" deliberately, because that is a method of transport in which you look fixedly in one direction while actually trying to move your craft as smartly as possible in the other.

Any President who sets out on this devious course is almost bound to be attacked simultaneously by the doves, who say that he is not moving fast enough, and by the hawks, who condemn him for starting to scuttle at all. There have been some such assaults on President Nixon. But I believe that a President Humphrey who moved at Nixon's present pace would have been far more bitterly attacked by both sides, and that this could have done great new harm to America's society. If a President Humphrey had delivered Nixon's recent speeches, still keeping the war and the draft going, the demonstrations by the doves of the moratorium would surely have been less peaceful. Left-wing Americans would have felt some despair that even a left-wing government judged it could not move faster. With Nixon they have felt some hidden relief (although they are certainly not going to express it) that a right-wing government has moved as fast as it has done in starting to get out from under what is now recognized as an impossible commitment.

Even more notably, Nixon has not yet stirred up any dangerous backlash from the right. Historically, this is a remarkable achievement. After all, the greatest power ever known in the world looks at present (Christmas, 1969) as if it is about to lose a war for the first time in its proud history, and at the hands of small, poor, inefficient, and slightly ridiculous North Vietnam. When other great powers have lost wars against all their expectations, they have often suffered a relapse into some sort of prickly right-wing nationalism. A recent example was Gaullist France, which was born because France lost its war in Algeria. Be-

fore that there was the more dreadful example of Germany
when it lost its war in 1918 (after having regarded itself
as invincible since Bismarck); and fearful jingoist events
threatened in late Victorian British society during the first
year of the Boer war, when Britain seemed to be losing.
But I can see little danger at present of the Vietnam tragedy
leading to any upsurge of belligerent nationalism in the
United States. Under the quiet, unexcitable and unexciting
President Nixon, the worry is rather that America's foreign
policy may pass into a stage of rather languid disengage-
ment during the 1970s.

Internally, these same qualities of the Nixon era seem to
me to have done a little—a very little—to tone down the
harshness of the black rebellions and the "radical" students'
riots; and they have done quite a lot to defuse the conservative backlash against that rebellion and those riots. This
latter containment has been aided by the fact that Vice
President Agnew has made himself the spokesman of a
mild and watery sort of conservative reaction. Ordinary
conservatives have found Agnewism a respectable sort of
conservatism to applaud, and only extraordinary liberals
can consider it a really cancerous growth that threatens
American society (although some humorless liberal American newspapers have tried to pretend that it is).

On political matters, therefore, I think the Nixon administration has done fairly well in an exceptionally difficult situation. Unhappily, in economic matters I think the
Nixon administration has done unexpectedly badly, in what
is really a fairly easy situation. In the survey that follows,
it will be seen that I argued that the Nixon administration
should go flat out for economic growth, even if its leaders
thought that this involved the risk of the continuance of in-

ix

flation. I expected them to ignore this gratuitous advice, and they did—but to a greater extent than they themselves were saying they meant to in March of 1969.

The original backroom objective of the administration was to reach a real annual growth rate of about 3 per cent at the end of 1969, and it thought that by then an annual inflation rate of about 3 per cent would be associated with this. Instead, it looks as if real growth at the end of 1969 had dropped to about nil (I write before the detailed figures are available), and inflation has obviously been proceeding at a much higher annual rate.

Looking into 1970 from the end of 1969, it seems odd to judge that America is still caught in a demand-pull inflation; it is caught in a cost-push inflation, and it is a mistake to try to fight that with anti-demand-pull weapons. On most grounds of orthodox economic analysis, there ought to have been an easing of monetary and other economic policy during the last quarter of 1969. This does not mean that America is necessarily likely to plunge into a real recession. The sophistication of the administration's economic advisers is great enough to lessen the risk of that. In addition, businessmen have caught on to this fact sufficiently well to be still keeping up their plans for fixed investment (a fact that some in the administration, quite wrongly, attribute to the "inflation-mindedness" of American business); businessmen are also, thank heavens, so far keeping up their rate of imports and most of their rate of employment. In particular, social consciousness is making American businessmen less likely to sack black American workers than they were at the beginning of previous slowdowns in economic growth below potential capacity.

Some of the worst usual effects of a slowdown have therefore not been felt. But America in the last half of 1969 has still unnecessarily sacrificed economic growth and thus real resources that it could have devoted to many urgent needs of its society. I am afraid that I believe that the main fault here has been a strictly personal failing of President Nixon himself. I still consider that his Council of Economic Advisers, under Paul McCracken, has been near the top rank of American CEAs. But I quote in this survey the perceptive view of Walter Heller that, for the CEA to succeed, "access not just to the person but to the mind of the President is crucial"; I also quote Heller's description of how concepts such as that of aiming at 4 per cent annual growth "were imprinted with the Presidential seal in Kennedy's first year and thereby became administration policy." I do not think that any economic policies have been imprinted with the Presidential seal during Nixon's first year, because I now do not think that Nixon normally imprints that sort of seal; he is more likely to hit at things with his flappers. I am also now more inclined than ten months ago to repeat the warning that "I have a lurking suspicion that Richard Nixon will not prove to possess John Kennedy's clear mind about how mechanisms can be set up," and to be worried about the way in which a sensible economic policy in America can be temporarily stifled by a bloated committee system. I hasten to say that if ever a real threat of serious recession did arise in America, then I still think that President Nixon has an able enough mind to react fairly quickly, and I am confident that his main economic advisers would then come into their own and get him to implement broadly the right policies. But in years when crisis does not actually threaten, I think the machinery of economic government under the Nixon administration is going to be less dynamic than I had hoped in March, 1969.

This is a pity. In social policy, the Nixon administra-

xi

tion has moved in many of the right directions. If ever the administration got back on a proper growth path, one which gave it an adequate "fiscal dividend," then I am inclined to believe it would be wiser than the last two administrations in deciding the most cost-effective ways in which the social welfare share of that fiscal dividend should be spent. But, in this first year of office, it has kept that fiscal dividend at a level smaller than it need have been.

Apart from these points, my conclusions of ten months ago remain unchanged.

NORMAN MACRAE
December, 1969

Contents

NORMAN MACRAE, the deputy editor of The Economist, has been visiting the United States. Part of his report below is concerned with what all other countries ought to be learning from this greatest and most successful economy, which will probably reach a gross national product of a trillion dollars in 1971 and in which average family income by the end of the century is likely to be a fantastic $25,000 a year. But his report necessarily also examines why social policy in the United States has recently gone so very badly wrong, and speculates on the dangers that could now send it even more wrong. In the opening chapter, which borrows its title from a Bagehotian phrase, he begins by assessing the decent-minded, but not large-minded, men of President Nixon's administration, who have now inherited an awesome responsibility to be at once a political sedative, a social healer and the leader of mankind's last important economic advance. Only parts of these roles will come naturally to them. [Prefatory note that appeared in The Economist.]

The
Mormons
Oust
the
Pugilists

The United States in this last third of the twentieth century is the place where man's long economic problem is ending, but where his social problems still gape. On any rational view, the enormous fact of that approach to economic consummation should rivet all attention. It is almost certainly the most momentous news-story so far in the history of the world. But people in the United States are at present wracked by the stretching to snapping point of too many of their temporary social tensions, so that this society which represents man's greatest secular achievement sometimes seems to be on the edge of a national nervous breakdown.

The theme of this survey is going to be that the cautious, conservative, Christian men of President Richard Nixon's administration have inherited, from the days of John Kennedy's new frontier, a continuing economic miracle; but also, from the wreck of Lyndon Johnson's great society, the devil of a sociological mess. The two main features of that sociological mess are an urban-

Negro-crisis of daunting proportions, and a ridiculous misorganisation of the structure of power that is desirable for a peaceful society.

The Nixon administration therefore finds itself simultaneously on man's last march before the borders of a material Utopia, and also at the unquiet limit of the modern world. This is a bewildering place for a team of relatively conservative lawyers and public servants, but relatively liberal businessmen and bankers, to be. The Nixon government proves to be an admirably open administration to newsgatherers. I was granted interviews with virtually all the main economic decision-makers within a week of alighting on Washington, and I suppose that I must now repay with a journalist's usual impoliteness by analysing my generous hosts. For, if we really are at a crossroads of human history, it is important for all of us to ponder who has just got up there in the driving seat of our leading van.

God is alive again

Compared with the last Republican administration in 1952–60, a visit with the Nixon economic team provides a foreign journalist with an emotionally restful experience. There are no real troglodytes among it. In Eisenhower days, one met people in the very top Treasury jobs who thought that the only function of a true Treasury man was to balance the budget—come recession, slump, or whatever. What came was therefore recession, and if the 1950s had not been a time of advancing technological revolution it could conceivably have been a slump. In the Nixon administration, by contrast, understanding of what is still oddly called the new economics appears to be virtually universal, and in just enough of the right offices it is also deep. This does not mean that only the faces and public relations have changed since the days of LBJ.

Compared with the Johnson administration, a main impression is that the Mormons have taken over from the social pugilists. Religion is an unexpectedly intrusive force in Mr Nixon's new Washington. If there were a sudden economic crisis tomorrow, requiring resolute American action before the weekend, at least two of the five men whose decisions would be most important would first retire into a backroom to pray for guidance from God. Fortunately, it is believed that His advice would belong to the emollient school, without being dictatorially rigid about anything. Among the more worldly economists in Mr Nixon's team, there is an atmosphere of relaxed intellectual opposition to big government, plus perhaps, in one or two places, a rather less relaxed resentment that for eight years it has tended to be assumed that all creative thinkers are Democrats; but nobody is likely to propose anything extreme just to prove the reverse. Among the longer-term politicians (whom I generally did not meet), there is an emphasis on being undoctrinaire, which obviously could mean opportunist or indecisive;

3

but it is fair to report that at the end of February President Nixon himself was still unfeignedly (I think) revered by all members of his team, including by some whose reverence I found slightly surprising.

Small-minded decency

Some of the team's answers to specific questions do raise eyebrows. When asked "what do you regard as the most difficult problem you have inherited?," the most frequent reply was "to stop inflation." It is blazingly certain that history will not regard 1968's 4 per cent rise in consumer prices as that beastly year's worst contribution to the American scene. When asked his ideas about welfare policy towards Negroes, one replied:

4

> The American Indian has been sadly damaged as a person by living off welfare handouts for many years. We have now for the first time Negro families who have lived off welfare handouts through three generations. My personal view is that it is important not to cause the Negro to follow down the American Indian's road.

This is not, to be fair, the rationalised meanness of a hard right-wing heart that at first hearing it certainly sounds. It is an old accusatory theme of liberal American historians and sociologists that white immigrants gave the

American Indian money, and did not train him for jobs. Nobody should underestimate the honourable impulses of the new administration even—or perhaps especially—when its members are saying the damnedest things.

Where the Johnson team saw the present American tragedy in terms of underprivilege and poverty crying out for justice in a land of plenty, Nixon men are apt to see it in terms of a melancholy diminution of faith in church and family and in all the true old institutions of America's once friendly neighbourhood life. One of the most determined claims of the men who have moved into the White House's executive office building is that "this Nixon administration" really will show a keenness for good government as an institution, in senses where they clearly feel that Lyndon Johnson devalued it. "We are showing our readiness to bring about good government even when it hurts our own people," they say: citing President Nixon's decision at long last to make local post office appointments on grounds of merit, instead of party patronage, and his willingness to move at least part of the way forward to block some tax loopholes through which certain well-publicised millionaires were last year able, quite legally, to persuade the revenue authorities that they were poor chaps with no taxable incomes at all.

"Sure," said a cross Democratic friend, to whom I recounted this earnest good house-cleaning intention, "Nero fiddled while Rome was burning. Now Nixon will be closing tax fiddles while Washington does so." Two years ago I would have been as horrified as he obvi-

5

ously is to see these decent-minded, but not large-minded, men come to top power in the world. Now I am inclined only half to share his apprehensions, and half actually to welcome the new team. In explaining this second half, starting with the next chapter, I expect to be accused of illiberalism.

Black
Ruin?

If you create wealth in America, it fructifies. If you create power groups, they usually go corrupt. President Kennedy's administration understood the first point; President Johnson's forgot the second. Now America has a grim race war, which is going to lead to white backlash.

America's most urgent task today is to solve its urban crisis: by which I mean, bluntly, to hurry forward by all available means the suburbanisation of the hordes of sometimes socially inadequate Negroes who have swarmed into the rotting ghettos near to so many of its cities' hearts. The United States has often before seen a large influx of particular racial or ethnic groups into particular parts of its big towns: of Irish, Jews, Italians, Germans, Swedes, and what Vice President Agnew no longer calls Polacks, to name but a few. Such inflows have not been without their problems—as was shown, all too desperately, by the lush sprouting among yesterday's urban poor, the Italians, of gangster mobs and political bosses of the crudest sorts. But eventually the great mass of each such group has been marvellously absorbed into middle class respectability, and into suburban love of "nice things," by the great healing power of accumulating wealth in America's very decent upper bourgeois society.

The Negroes present a tougher urban problem, because there are so many of them (one-ninth of the population), and because they are starting without the immigrants' "American dream" shining in their eyes. They have three centuries worth of just and terrible grievances smouldering there instead. But the great economic growth started under John Kennedy in the early 1960s was genuinely at last bringing major and much overdue advances in income and status towards black Americans. It is a pity that a minor mishandling of this economic growth in the middle Johnson years, 1965–67, caused a small inflation to start too, which the Republicans now regard as the great American crisis; but this small economic error was not the real trouble. The real trouble has been Mr Johnson's great society's great sociological failure. The essence of this is still not generally understood abroad, because it is ritualistically misunderstood at home by good-hearted American liberals.

Again and again, the United States should have learned from its history that, if you create wealth in America, it fructifies; but, if you create power groups in America, they go corrupt. The great society's projects should have been directed towards discouraging the growth of power groups; instead, at least to some extent (as we shall see), some positively encouraged them.

Now the most nerve-racking thing has happened. The Negro community has sprouted a large charade cast of tough so-called "black power" leaders, with a highly developed sense of the dramatic as their most common characteristic. None of them so far has a real national following, but all are fighting for local followings, with violence as a weapon in those fights that is never very far in the wings. Many of these "leaders" are, inevitably, of an intimidatory, unlovable, lower middle class, lurid fascist type; and, of course, crime is going to be increasingly associated with what they do, as has happened with such American urban political movements before. Moreover, all this is occurring at a time when a temporary and rather extraordinary toleration by the American people of flamboyant violence is almost certainly about to turn to a harsh white intolerance of it.

9

Violence nears its term

The reasons for the temporary toleration of violence by many American white liberals in the past five years were:

(1) The battle for civil rights in the southern United States in the early 1960s was won through "sit-ins" and other demonstrations against local authorities who were not obeying federal law. Northern liberals (indeed, almost all the world) approved of these sit-ins, and a very evanescent period of regarding demonstrators as probably beautiful people began.

(2) The United States has been fighting a war in Vietnam by means of an army compulsorily conscripted

through the draft. A substantial minority of the country has opposed this war, and they have included a majority of the young university students who have been under the shadow of possible conscription, as well as a large number of the intellectual leaders of America. No other democratic country has successfully fought unpopular, and arguably imperialist, wars far from home with forced enrolment to its colours. France tried it with a war just across the Mediterranean in Algeria, and look what was the result. Britain could not have fought the Boer war seventy years ago with a conscript army (in which sons of Fabians and Lloyd-George liberals could be compelled to serve) unless it was ready to face some disturbances. These anti-Vietnam-war demonstrators in the United States therefore attracted considerable sympathy, even when they became a bit rougher than passive sitters-down.

The reasons why this toleration is about to be replaced in America by intolerance are:

(1) With the cooling of the Vietnam issue, student riots in America are at present frequently run by black students, in support of black power demands, though usually with help from the largely white and nominally left-wing Students for a Democratic Society, who join in for the revolutionary thrill. These black students' battles and SDS-sponsored riots are making war, not love. I describe on page 88 a sickening instance of intimidation and violence which I witnessed at one of America's most famous

and liberal universities. Some (not all) of these actions by black-uniformed black power students and "radical" white students this winter moved right over the border of what humanists should tolerate, and invited the most direct comparison with the way that Hitler's brownshirts operated in the Weimar republic: except that these youths—however much they may have thought they were talking democracy—were in practice using harassment of elderly liberal or conservative academics as the means of excitement of their own and their followers' thug instincts, where Hitler used Jews. Hitherto, liberal academics have been the biggest-hearted supporters of the militant American Negroes' and radicals' case. This is now rather unlikely to last for long.

× (2) The crime rate among the present generation of   *11*
young urban Negroes is proving to be very high. An example in the liberal Kerner report showed one Negro ghetto to have proportionately 35 times as many serious crimes against the person as a white suburb of the same city. This is not at all surprising in view of the conditions in which some dwellers in the ghettos have to live. Indeed the really terrible charge against rich white American society lies precisely in this: that, because of the culture that white America has been mainly responsible for shaping, 2 million decent black American families— members of a very churchgoing, and basically rather gentle, community—are living in the city centres today with the hopeless and sickening knowledge that their

kids have an above-average risk of turning delinquent. In addition, most Negro youths' crimes are naturally against other Negroes. In America as a whole a black woman has a 3.7 times higher probability of being raped than a white woman, and any Negro has at least a 3.5 times higher probability of being robbed.

Inevitably, however, this high black delinquency rate has stirred thoughts less self-condemnatory than these among most white Americans. Together with the white flight to the suburbs, which has made Negroes so large a proportion of the total population of many city areas (66 per cent in Washington), it means that the centres of many of America's biggest cities have become extremely nervy places to walk about at night. As an immediate and unheroic personal story: I am typing the first draft of this in my Washington hotel room that looks across Lafayette Square at the beautiful portico of the White House and the bulbous ugliness of its executive office building. A lot of my interviews this week have been in that executive office building. When one has ended after dark my progress over the 100 yards back from there to here has been at an undignified scuttle across the centre of the world.

Nobody should underestimate the effect on a people of this feeling of insecurity and terror in places which they used to regard as the showpieces of their proud civilisation. Meanwhile, white Americans fear (probably rightly) that the "black power" ideology may make some

Negro youths feel that robberies and assaults on white women and other passers-by are almost a noble act of black revolution.

The result of all this is going to be a white backlash. The concern of all humane people should be to limit it. Probably the main danger is not of trigger-happy white vigilantes, but of the political pendulum swinging back far. If a President Hubert Humphrey had been elected last November, trying to be liberal-minded in all of his utterances and some of his deeds, my guess is that a representative of the backlash—perhaps of the Governor Reagan type—would have won the Republican nomination in 1972, and probably have gained the White House. That is one reason for half-welcoming the fact that Mr Humphrey did not succeed.

13

The key is growth

What America needed last November, in short, was to take a political sedative, but also to maintain the pace of general economic advance which alone can bring the Negro through to the decent bourgeois life. What the country has got with Mr Nixon is presumably a political sedative all right. At times (though not always) during my visit to Washington I was inclined to say that few things could be more sedative than this crashing lot of bores. The danger is that the new mixture may contain too much of an economic sedative too. The expressed policy of the new team is to introduce a mild curb on economic growth in order to check inflation. Any such curb is liable to fall much more heavily upon black workers than upon white ones. The present 3.4 per cent general unemployment rate means that only 1½ per cent of adult white males are out of work, and it is said that the recent "ruinous rise in inflationary pressures" will continue unless this rate is increased. But a general 5 per cent unemployment rate in America would be likely to mean an average 10 per cent of jobless among all Negroes, 15 per cent in the ghettos, and probably over 30 per cent among Negro teenagers. The administration might then find that it was exerting its mild curb by mildly holding a black panther by the tail. This is not a recommended procedure in America's cities for the next few years.

14

This survey will deal with economic policy and prospects first, and indeed mainly. Partly, this is because, if one visits the greatest country on earth, one does best to study most closely the sector connected with one's own normal professional interests. But there are two other reasons. The first is that I have become more than ever convinced that it is only through continued economic growth, leading to suburbanisation of the Negro, that the present neurosis of the world's first trillionaire can be removed. The second reason is, for a European, more selfish; but it takes over from this point on as the principal theme of this survey.

A mirror to our futures

The great interest for a foreign visitor to America today is not that he is sitting in at another showing of a sad sociological muddle played back again from America's past. It is that he is able to peer forward through a priceless telescope at the economic forces that are most likely to influence all other countries' futures. The main historical fact about America today is not that it presents the all-too-usual spectacle of a major human story being badly mishandled. It is that it is demonstrating the most productive use of resources ever achieved by man— and this at a time when knowledge (which is transmittable between people) has become by far the most important of those economic resources.

Do not let us lose for a moment a sense of excitement at the extraordinary prospect of achieving material sufficiency for all, within our children's lifetimes, if only we settle down to the obviously feasible task of imitating what America is already doing organisationally, managerially, industrially. Do not let us be so supine as to suppose that we cannot learn from its achievements in these fields, while at the same time determining not to repeat its sociological mistakes. Here, in the economic experience of the United States of America, is the written book. This is the royal law. These are the lively oracles of Mammon's Own Country.

15

Mammon's
Own
Country

American workers are approximately twice as productive as European ones. Why? And will this last?

The big story in the United States is the approach to economic consummation. Median family income there is now well over $8,000 a year, and even for oppressed black Americans it is close to $5,500. This last figure contrasts with Britain's average family income in 1967 of $4,414, if one converts at the $2.40 exchange rate. But the really important inheritance from the 1960s is that most informed Americans now appear to be confident that their country knows how to go on expanding its real gross national product by between 3 and 5 per cent per annum compound. In the next 15 years, when the labour force should be expanding by between 1 and 2 per cent a year, they should be able to get an average annual growth in GNP of around or over 4 per cent quite easily. Simply by applying existing technology, sober corporate planners and backroom government projectionists presume that America will be able to push its median family income to about $25,000 a year, in terms of today's prices, by around the turn of the century—say, by about the time that any baby born this week is in the main family-rearing stages of his own working life.

This is not only by far the farthest man has advanced in all his long struggle from unending hunger and toil to the threshold of comfort and leisure. As a definition of arrival at comfort and leisure, it will quite simply do. The trail from here to material sufficiency has therefore been mapped out, and the main job of economists now is to read that map. I would say: especially in north-west Europe, which is the next large group of people in line behind the United States in industrial maturity and income per head.

17

The gap and the haul

Any European looking at the American economy has to ask two questions. The aggravating one is: why are these people producing nearly twice as many goods and services per person employed as we Europeans do, and are America's advantages capable of being copied? The rest of this chapter will discuss this. It is going to come to a slightly-better-than-pessimistic conclusion. I think that a large part of America's productivity lead is unfortunately due to the sort of factor which any numerate analyst hates to find exists—namely, some vaguely definable special go-getting urge in the culture of the majority of the American people—but I will also suggest that Europe ought to be particularly well placed to narrow some of this gap during the next stage of its educational and technical advance.

This leads to the second question: namely, is the road which Europe is now likely to travel, and which America has traversed before, a stretch in which politicians of moderate competence will find the management of economic policy very difficult? Here one can be an out-and-out optimist. Recent experience in the United States has fortunately suggested that the management of economic policy in a near-mature economy is almost unbelievably easy: so much so that even the extraordinarily inefficient American governmental machine has not managed to muff it. Among advanced countries, only the even more inefficient British governmental machine so far has. The quite clear lessons of America's recent governmental experience in economic matters are discussed in four chapters starting on page 29. Meanwhile this chapter will return to analysing the existing productivity gap.

Dr Denison's residual

The analysis has to begin, as so often for any international analyst, with the superbly brave statistical compilations of Dr Edward F. Denison, America's master-economist on this subject. Dr Denison calculated* that in 1960 real national income per person employed in north-west Europe was either 46 or 59 per cent of that in the United States, according to whether one values production at European or American price weights. Both are equally justifiable. The layman can decently translate this as saying that the average north-west European is only about half as productive as the average American. Britain was at this time dead equal to the north-west European average.

If one uses the index that puts Europe (and thus Britain) at 59 per cent of America's productivity, then Dr Denison's statistical researches suggested:

(1) About 10 of the 41 percentage points in this "gap" are due to the fact that the Americans have more capital equipment per worker in industry; indeed, on some price weightings, approximately twice as much. (As another form of what some would call "capital," America gains through having a more educated labour force, but Dr Denison judged this to be virtually cancelled by the fact that the labour force in America spends a 4 per cent shorter time at work, largely because a lot of the working married women do only part-time jobs.) Most European countries, although not Britain, are now cutting down the big American lead in capital equipment by devoting a higher proportion of GNP to investment than the Americans do.

19

* See "Why Growth Rates Differ?" By Edward F. Denison, assisted by Jean-Pierre Poullier. Brookings Institution, 1967.

(2) About another 5 percentage points of America's lead can be ascribed to "economies of scale" in its larger factories, and another 2½ per cent on average to Europe's misallocation of manpower to low productivity occupations (especially its uneconomic hordes in peasant farming and small shopkeeping). The European countries, which used to be most over-peasanted—including Italy, France, and Germany—have recently been getting their labour off the land very fast; Britain, which drew its excess labour off the land long ago, has not been able to enjoy this extra source of growth.

(3) The statistics suggest that only minor gains, generally of less than 1 percentage point, came from other American advantages—such as the greater willingness of American workers to do shift work (and thus use capital equipment more continuously) and the Americans' efficiency in fitting part-time workers into their industrial schedules (although, as suburban wives grow richer and school enrolment of teenagers increases, the research confirms that Britain has simply got to learn how to use part-time workers more frequently than now). Taken together, however, these other identifiable factors did not compensate for the American disadvantage in 1960 that the Eisenhower administration was running the economy at a wastefully high level of unemployment.

(4) It followed that Dr Denison believed that nearly 24 points of America's 41 point lead in productivity over north-west Europe, and over 29 points of its 41 point

20

lead over Britain, could only be ascribed to such residual factors as Europe's and Britain's "lag in the application of knowledge" and "general inefficiency." Dr Denison found it especially disturbing that north-west Europe's real output per worker in 1960 was only approximately the same as America's in 1925, although by 1960 Europe's workers were much better educated than American workers had been in 1925—and had of course a far more advanced technology to draw on. The implication is that there is some long-standing, history-given, go-getting element in America's culture which Europeans and others have been unable to imitate. This factor might be called "Denison's residual," and it is incumbent on any European researcher into America to see if he thinks he can spot the bug.   *21*

Computers are coming—hurrah, hurrah

I am convinced in my own mind that Denison's residual does exist; and that I know what it sounds and smells like. It can best be described as the greater air of professionalism which runs through all ranks of American society: the greater instinct among ordinary individuals to say "now here is the problem, how can I solve it by a systematic approach?" A visiting economic journalist can get from a quite junior employee in America more sensible and detailed statistical answers about what a firm or financial organisation is trying to do, what appears to make it tick, and what sales and profits trends as between different products are, than he can usually get at very top levels in equivalent British corporations. It would be nice to pretend that this is because British firms are more shrewdly taciturn, but it is really because our top British businessmen (let alone their junior employees) often don't really know what their firms are aiming at in cost or efficiency or profit terms at any given time.

Moreover, this distinction runs right through the American and British communities, from the board room to the shop floor and the home. I had better illustrate this now by making an unsubstantiable statement which (because it will be unpopular) has every journalistic disadvantage, save only that it is true. If a management efficiency group were to time-motion study a scientifically significant sample of American and British housewives at the kitchen sink, it would almost certainly find that the average American housewife did her housework more than twice as efficiently (which means in less than half the time and with less than half the sweat) as the average British housewife, even if each of them had exactly the same labour-saving machines. The reason for this is that the American housewife, although she will be surprised to hear this, instinctively works out in her head for each chore some rough approximation of what modern businessmen call a critical path analysis. She works out what she will want where, and when she will require to use it, while the average British housewife just meanders.

This may make Americans sound like unimitatable geniuses, and Europeans sound like incurable dolts. Actually, in the field of top management, I am at present optimistic that Europe will start soon to narrow the large efficiency gap. There should be especial opportunities for Britain, which has the advantage of not only speaking the same language as America, but speaking some of the same new business efficiency jargon as well.

The particular cadres of management where Europe lags most grievously behind America are those which supply information to the decision-makers about what is going on in their business. This applies to cost accountants, salesmen, buyers, research departments of firms (which in America sometimes really do something, but in Britain seem to be working mainly on projects to justify themselves), marketing departments, and the like.

Two revolutions are about to engulf this greyest area of British and European business. First, the advance of higher education means that more of these types of jobs are going to be filled by university graduates, instead of by people who may very well have left school at 15. Secondly, and most fortunately, computers promise to be particularly important new tools in precisely these fields where in the pre-computer age American management was most strong and European management most weak. Immediately, it is true, the arrival of computers has caused America to widen the efficiency gap. This is because many American firms nowadays know how to use a computer efficiently, while European firms (some of whom have computerised the most extraordinarily inappropriate operations) generally do not. The use of computers by big British firms at present can best be compared to the prewar horror story about former slum dwellers who, when promoted into being council house tenants, tended to keep coal in the bath. But presumably the right use of the right tools will percolate through in time. It did quite quickly with baths.

24   The forgotten feudalism

Unfortunately computers are not going to come into the kitchen yet awhile. Even if data processing helps forward a managerial revolution in Europe, America's lead in go-getting culture among its ordinary working men and women will persist. But not, I would guess, by quite as big a margin as in the recent past. To explain this guess, one must theorise briefly on why the gap originally came about. Oddly, this may also throw some light on where multiracial America is now likely to go.

I suspect that the United States is one of the few countries where history is very important, chiefly because it has so little of it. You can forget everything before the 1860s. It was in the next three generations that the

United States was created, as the great grandfathers and grandfathers and fathers of most of today's leading men swarmed over from Europe in the great migrations. Cries the Statue of Liberty:

> Give me your tired, your poor,
> Your huddled masses, yearning to breathe free.
> The wretched refuse of your teeming shore,
> Send these, the hopeless tempest-tossed, to me

—in one of the finest first examples of brilliantly mendacious American public relations prose the connoisseur could hope to collect. What Europe sent instead was its best inaugurators, men who were to some extent rebelling against a social and economic inferiority which Europe's class system battened down on them, and heavily weighted with those who had enough ability to want to drive on and up.

We know from modern sociology that the influence of the home moulds a child far more closely than the influence of a school; and it is not therefore surprising that so many even of today's Americans are still twitching under the murmur of recent ancestral voices down these two or three bare generations. Those voices have been telling them that, in a land free of European residues of feudalism, all can and should drive forward to get things done—and should then hope in turn to see their children automatically surpass them in education, occupation, and prosperity. To this should be added the

25

point (heretical though it sounds to Europeans) that America had until recently a very good way of bringing up children in the home, breeding perky self-reliance; while Europe had a very bad one, expressing parental or class dominance.

The probability is that Europe will now manage to narrow the gap, partly because Europe really is becoming a progressively less feudal continent, and partly because of the appearance of two possible cankers on America's bud. One of these cankers is that the American Negro has never hitherto been fitted into the American dream of up-thrusting equal opportunity for all; he has been, as Dr James Tobin has put it, "the victim of America's own brand of feudalism and permitted inferiority." *

26 Now that he is rising, the American people are reacting with extraordinary political inefficiency to this emergence of an old-fashioned European class problem in their midst. I do not suggest that this is liable to tear the whole nation permanently apart. As the bumbling old European aristocracy eventually managed, by a limping process of condescension, concession, and reform, to integrate into a more-or-less decent society the 95 per cent hitherto-oppressed majority called the lower classes, it seems impossible to believe that the very educated modern American democracy can really fail eventually to integrate this last 11 per cent minority of its people called blacks. But it does now seem likely that the pres-

* In the Brookings Institution publication on problems before President Nixon, called *Agenda for the Nation*.

ent troubles will leave behind them some of the sediments that class struggles have left behind in European politics and moods. They have not been particularly useful sediments in Europe. The main one—the yielding of the left wing in politics from an attemptedly liberal party to an attemptedly social democratic one—often makes the election of either an anti-innovative or an inferiority-complexed government more frequent, and by this and other means impedes growth.

The other possible canker is the new attitude of some of America's youth. To the horror of old-fashioned Americans, the universities have recently been reporting a sharp increase among freshmen students in stated preferences for careers in teaching or government service, and a decline of interest in careers in business. This un-American trend is variously attributed by the older generation to the rebelliousness of youth, the fading down the years of those ancestral voices, or to the fact that this is the first generation that has been brought up from birth not on the principles of self-reliance, but on television-watching and the precepts of that treacherous Dr Spock. Once again, one doubts whether a whole course of history will really be changed by this. The most reasonable and moderate guess is perhaps that among these new generations there may be some diminution of America's hitherto superbly successful go-getting mentality—but the diminution is coming at a time when America has fortunately already nearly gone and got.

Ten years ago, it seemed doubtful whether the United

27

States would go and get quickly enough. The trouble was that, as has happened before in American history, its governmental mechanism for economic affairs seemed to be lagging so far behind the vibrant genius of its people. The great achievements of the 1960s are that this governmental mechanism has been reformed, and that the country has been set on a course of what many optimists now consider to be semi-automated economic expansion. I am inclined half to agree with this: in the sense that I believe that government management of American economic policy is now much more nearly idiot-proof. The next chapter discusses why.

Organisation
for
Growth

The Democratic administrations of the 1960s not only in-
augurated a modern macro-economic policy for America.
They have made it likely that the conventional wisdom will
regard what they have established as generally orthodox
from now on.

This survey will have some hard things to say of the
mistakes in the Democrats' social policy which the Nixon
administration needs to try to put right. But on macro-
economic policy it will cheer all the way for JFK, and
much of it for LBJ. By any reasonable measurement,
the Democratic administrations from 1961 to 1969 gave
the United States eight golden years of economic advance, with the greatest benefits going to the most poor.
    During the Eisenhower years of the 1950s the average
annual growth rate of real GNP had been under 2½
per cent; during the Kennedy-Johnson years it was over
5¼ per cent. On the eve of John Kennedy's inauguration, unemployment stood near to 7 per cent; by the
time of Lyndon Johnson's departure, it was down to 3.2

per cent. If one defines poverty (as some Americans do) at the rather generous figure of a family income of $3,000 a year in terms of 1967 prices, then in 1961 a horrifying 42.8 per cent of Negro families and 16.2 per cent of white families still fell below this line; by 1967 the figures were down to 27.1 per cent of Negro families and 12.5 per cent of white ones. These and other trends are shown in charts on pages 37 and 39, from which it will be seen that the performance was at least moderately respectable by more conservative criteria as well. The early years of Kennedy expansion were accompanied by an annual price inflation of under 1½ per cent (which is probably in reality equal to no inflation, because 1½ per cent a year may represent the understatement in the official price index of the annual improvement in the quality of goods on sale in American shops). It is true that prices went more wrong after late 1965, but that was because of certain correctable mistimings by the Johnson administration to which we will refer. And, although the balance of payments remained in deficit throughout, it was fairly consistently—and rather amazingly—a smaller deficit than was suffered by the Republicans in their last limping recessional years.

The greatest achievements, however, were a whole change of mood towards the economic opportunities before America, and a reorganisation of a mechanism of economic government that in the later Eisenhower years filled one with black despair. I can remember being

30

seriously told in Eisenhower's Washington during the 1958 recession that the whole of the country's unemployment rate (then 6.8 per cent) was due to structural maladjustments, and that the advance of automation meant that all mature industrial countries must accept in future that the less educated cohorts of their populations would be permanently unemployable. Any resort to reflation in these circumstances, it was said, would lead wholly to rises in prices and not at all to rises in real GNP.

This tendency to regard anyone less educated than oneself as obviously unemployable is a common and deplorable predilection in America's meritocratic society (as it is, incidentally, among Ministry of Labour civil servants in certain other countries); in my view, it is 31 dangerous in America even today because it blinds people to the wastefulness of present Negro underemployment. But in the last Eisenhower days this dirge about macro-economic policy being a useless tool against "structural" unemployment was soothing music to the ears even of decent-minded men who had wearily decided that it was impossible to get a macro-economic policy effected through the American machinery of government anyway: because nobody quite knew who could effect what decisions when. One group in the Republican administration—led by the then Vice President Nixon and his present adviser Professor Arthur Burns (see page 54) —did urge a tax cut just before 1958, when recession was clearly foreseeable and reflation was obviously needed. Their effort ran straight into the sand.

In America this year I made a point of visiting familiar figures from the Democratic days, to see how they viewed the battles and prospect ahead. Back in their university offices and bank parlours and executive suites and research institutes, they rest content. Walter Heller —who now sits in what is literally an academic tower in the University of Minnesota in far off Minneapolis, with his books having predictably far outrun his book cases, so that they march in alarmingly mounting piles round the floor—is on and off the record with statements about the Nixon administration of remarkable encouragement and benignity. And most of his erstwhile colleagues strike the same note. "It's going to be all right," said one, "we have left behind us some permanent concepts of modernity." That, I believe, was John Kennedy's miracle.

The institutionalised breakthrough

Thanks to the overruling of Vice President Nixon's sensible pleas for a tax cut in 1957, America ran into the recession years of 1958 and 1960, interspersed by 1959 which saw only the briefest of recoveries. In January, 1961, President Kennedy therefore inherited an economy which had at any rate had all cost-push inflation squeezed temporarily out of its system—but otherwise had little to recommend it. For it was also an economy with a large overseas payments deficit, and one in which the recession in incomes meant that tax revenue in 1961 was bound to be sluggish. The crazy conventions of the time therefore suggested that President Kennedy should set about cutting government expenditure again or even (as some in his own administration seriously advocated in mid-1961, for a time with sympathy from the President himself) put up tax rates. The prospect did not seem bright that inauguration day in 1961 that the Kennedy administration would prove to be the instrument that would establish, probably permanently, the rule of expertise, instead of prejudiced ignorance, in economic counsel at the centre of the world.

33

Yet that is what it did. John Kennedy's historic achievement, after a shaky start, is that he called into action the power of the Presidency to break a particular log-jam in the way of modernised economic policy (which is easy enough for a brief period, as Roosevelt showed in the New Deal), but then also formalised and institutionalised the breakthrough in ways—here lies his genius—that are likely to make conventional wisdom regard what he has established as generally orthodox from now on. To bring about these reforms, Kennedy (who in early 1961 was not himself an economic sophisticate) had first to acquire the understanding, second to establish the mechanism, and third to prove to have found the man.

A ride in a troika

He acquired the understanding by his extraordinary system of selecting advisers with very different views, and then choosing between them. Since in economic matters the knowledgeable Whigs could generally out-argue the emotional Tories, the highly intelligent Kennedy became a Whig before the end of 1961.

He established the governmental mechanism by taking conventional opinion for a ride in his "troika." This is a Russian term for a vehicle driven by a team of three horses running abreast, which cannot be very comfy for the horse in the middle. Kennedy's troika of advisers may originally have been mainly a device for ensuring that his liberal but Republican choice as Secretary of the Treasury, Douglas Dillon, had to keep running because he was flanked by the progressive Budget Director David Bell (later replaced by the equally progressive Kermit Gordon) and the pacesetting chairman of the Council of Economic Advisers, Professor Walter Heller. But this three-in-hand also proved to be the right-sized body for recommending decisions: not only at the top level where the three principals met, but also in committees lower down at deputy and technical levels (where there were usually four members, because Walter Heller's council of economic advisers managed to push in an extra one) .

It has been a major governmental lesson of recent

34

years that very small gatherings of this kind are much more decisive in economic affairs than the appalling British system of large interdepartmental committees of civil servants from all the departments and non-departments that have to be presumed to be interested, so that representatives of the Board of Trade, and of the Ministry of Overseas Development, and of Mr Benn's Ministry of Technology, and of Mr Shore's pathetically underemployed rump, all have to be given an opportunity to cross something out. The point is important, because there is some danger (see page 54) that President Nixon may try to restore some decisions of government to larger cabinet committees.

35

The Heller doctrines

Finally, President Kennedy found the man for his economic revolution in Walter Heller, the tall, drawling professor from Minnesota who reminds one irresistibly of the film star James Stewart playing some country hick who comes to Washington and accidentally changes the history of the world—with the remarkable rider that probably Heller actually did. Behind the several myths about him, Walter Heller is a rather orthodox Keynesian economist (even a slightly conservative one, in that he believes fairly explicitly in Phillips curves), who has the sort of mind that likes to think rather specifically in terms of figures, and is therefore rarely ambiguous in what he says. This happened to be exactly the right mixture of numerate economic sophistication and literate political unsophistication at exactly the right time. Two of the concepts sponsored during Heller's period at the Council of Economic Advisers became of crucial importance.

The first concept was the "GNP gap." The simple calculation here was that the economy was running in 1961 at an average unemployment rate of 6.7 per cent, and the average utilisation rate of manufacturing capacity was only 78.5 per cent. If unemployment was brought down to 4 per cent, it was calculated that gross national product could be increased by $40 billion a year, so the right way to bring unemployment down to 4 per cent was for the government to see that $40 billion of extra demand (after allowance for multiplier effects) was created in order to fill this "GNP gap." The enunciation of this doctrine led to a great outcry from conservative people that the creation of anything like this amount of new demand would cause grave inflation, not growing prosperity. When it caused growing prosperity instead, the notion of talking about a GNP gap at times of underemployment passed into respectability.

The second major new concept was that of the "full employment budget surplus." Put simply, the original argument here was that the nominal budget deficit in 1961 was going to be around $3½ billion; but if the country had been earning those extra billions a year because of full employment, then at least some $8 bil-

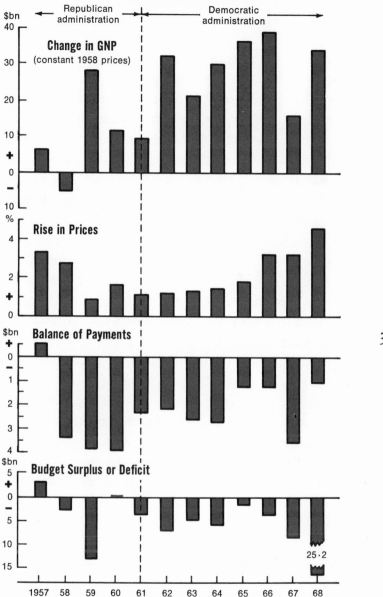

ECONOMIC INDICATORS

← Republican administration | Democratic administration →

Change in GNP (constant 1958 prices)

$bn
40
30
20
10
+
0
–
10

Rise in Prices

%
4
2
+
0

Balance of Payments

$bn
+
0
–
1
2
3
4

Budget Surplus or Deficit

$bn
5
+
0
–
5
10
15

25·2

1957 58 59 60 61 62 63 64 65 66 67 68

37

NOTES: Each year's change in gross national product shown in billions of dollars at constant (1958) prices. Prices shown as percentage point increases on 1957–59 = 100. Balance of payments deficit or surplus shown on liquidity basis, and budget deficit or surplus on "unified budget" basis.

lion of extra tax revenue would automatically have been gathered in from these extra incomes, so that it was fair to say that the administration was aiming at what would have been a budget surplus if the country had full employment. The traditional American equation of any budget deficit with original sin had always been based on lack of knowledge, so that this inspired sophistry served very well for people who could now say "on one definition, you know, the budget is sound."

To this, Kennedy's economic advisers added the concepts of "fiscal dividend" and "fiscal drag." As America's economy moves along the potential output path of 4 per cent expansion a year, and with reasonably steady prices, the federal tax system generates an increase in tax revenues of about 6 per cent a year (this greater proportional rise in tax receipts than in incomes occurs because, among other things, the income tax system is progressive). The Heller doctrine is that unless this automatic growth in revenue—or "fiscal dividend"—is offset by reductions in tax rates or deliberate increases in government expenditure, it will act as a "fiscal drag" by siphoning off income and pushing the economy towards recession.

Why CEA worked

This teaching has now passed into the conventional wisdom of American government. Not indeed of Congress, which has the nominal final say on spending authorisations and tax rates; but, as Kennedy saw better than

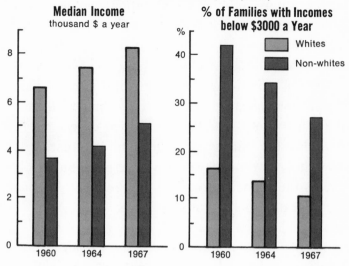

FAMILY INCOMES (1967 prices)

Median Income
thousand $ a year

% of Families with Incomes below $3000 a Year

Whites

Non-whites

39

Lyndon Johnson, there are ways of getting round that. It is in the civil service and among Republican, as well as Democratic, recruits to the executive that conversion seems almost complete. Down the long corridors of fiscal power the apostles of an ever-balanced budget, who so terrified any visiting economist in 1958, have been replaced by successors intent on working out how to spend or remit the fiscal dividend. America now has a mechanism for expansionist economic policies written into the efficient part of its inefficient constitution. The result is that, unless there is some awful muddle in mone-tary policy, America is unlikely to have a really lasting recession between now and the end of the century.

This has been an extraordinary achievement in popular—and almost subliminal—education by the Council of Economic Advisers (hereafter called CEA) during its greatest decade. It is important for students of government to understand why this rather odd body works. On the face of things, this team of 15 to 20 highly trained professional economists—only three of them on the council itself—would seem likely to degenerate into a fan club for writing memoranda to one another, because they have no departmental responsibilities. The secret is the council's access to the President. To quote one of Walter Heller's own speeches:

> *It is the business with and for the President that makes the standard 80- to 90-hour week of Council members productive, rewarding, and memorable. Access not just to the person but to the mind of the President is crucial. The Council's major instrument of access to a modern President is the development of economic concepts, targets, and policies that fit his philosophy and further his high purposes—indeed, sometimes give concrete shape to those purposes, as did the concepts of economic potential and the GNP gap and the targets of 4 per cent unemployment and 4½ per cent annual growth. All of these were imprinted with the Presidential seal in Kennedy's first year and thereby became Administration policy.*

40

The importance of the revolution that has been effected can perhaps best be seen by the sad contrast with other parts of the economic governing machine, where such formalisation and institutionalisation of modernised economic concepts have not quite taken place.

Two lights that failed

The two most disappointing sectors of the American economic scene today are the two that appeared least bad ten years ago, but have since then escaped thorough organisational reform. The first field is America's foreign economic policy, in which the Eisenhower administration had been rather liberal (thanks partly in the later years to his Under Secretary of State, who was none other than Douglas Dillon). In President Kennedy's early years, effective management of America's foreign economic policy devolved partly on the brilliant Under Secretary of the Treasury Robert Roosa; and Bob Roosa's policies were quite the right ones for the time. Since the continental Europeans were unwilling to create more international liquidity in formal dress, he set about creating it in informal habits: through the great network of swap credits which have been the international financial system's temporary salvation.

By definition, however, this amelioration by stealth could not leave a corpus of reforming concepts behind it. The institutional mechanism was also cloudier, since international economic policy was not decided through the troika and its small three-man or four-man committees; it was apt to be the responsibility of wider

41

committee meetings of civil servants and central bank officials from the Federal Reserve instead. After Mr Roosa's departure, the system decayed, despite the personal ability in the last years of Under Secretary Deming. The situation was not helped by the fact that Mr Henry Fowler, who became Secretary of the Treasury in 1965, did not have Mr Dillon's experience in international affairs. America's foreign economic policy since the mid-1960s has been an untidy mess of passions (such as the mysterious determination that gold must on no account be deemed to be more expensive than $35 an ounce) and committee compromise. The result was that the outbreak of the Bonn crisis last November found the United States with no visible contingency plan whatever.

42

The incoming Nixon administration has some brighter ideas in this field. Most of its thinkers—for example, in the CEA—are strongly in favour of helping to move the world towards a system of more flexible exchange rates. But it has not found any mechanism in being for implementing a foreign economic policy, and I have a lurking suspicion that Richard Nixon will not prove to possess John Kennedy's clear mind about how mechanisms can be set up. When I was in Washington in February, Mr Paul Volcker was in Mr Deming's old job as the relevant Under Secretary of the Treasury; but delicate questions about where powers of decision would be likely to lie, when and if a new Bonn-type crisis breaks, got differing answers. This is usually a bad sign.

The other sadness today is the Federal Reserve. In 1958 it used to be a refreshment to escape from interviews in the Eisenhower departments to interviews in this intelligent central bank. Perhaps what has happened in the years between is not that the Federal Reserve has got worse, but that everybody else has got better. The Kennedy-Johnson formula for dealing with the proudly independent Fed was merely to put some bright people on its seven-man board as vacancies fell due; plus a less formal attempt to bring it into closer contact with the troika, so that it is common parlance in Washington nowadays to talk about issues "on which the troika becomes a quadriad."

The brutal fact remains that any economic journalist from Britain who visits the Federal Reserve today feels   43
with a sinking heart that he is almost back in London. All those people beavering away in the Federal Reserve are not working to scientific concepts (like the GNP gap) or to a man (like the President) ; they are working to a committee. The main committee is the Open Market Committee, which consists of the seven governors of the Federal Reserve Board and the presidents of the twelve Federal Reserve district banks (of whom only five may vote). It seems to an outsider to show many of the failings of the system of large interdepartmental committees which fails to run the economic policy of Britain: so that policy directives are not expressed in clear language, but are usually trimmed so as to smooth ruffled feelings aroused by reminders about who has

been proved allegedly right or allegedly wrong since the last meeting. In Britain, the next stage usually becomes an intermittent sticking to, and then unsticking from, guns which are fired most unitedly not at the real problems of the national economy, but at any measures which could imply truckling to viewpoints of critics who have particularly annoyed the system. Some of the same distracting habits seem to be present in the Federal Reserve today, as the guns blaze most determinedly and confusedly at both left-wing "inflationists" and the right-wing Professor Milton Friedman (let alone at any maverick who says "raise the price of gold"). We will be returning to these criticisms of the Federal Reserve later, when the reader can judge how far he thinks we have been too rude.

44

Unfortunately, there was a third gap in the decision-making process that John Kennedy left behind. There was no connecting link, except the person of the President himself, between those concerned with economic policy and those in other departments of government who could greatly affect the matters with which economic policy would have to deal. After the assassination at Dallas, Lyndon Johnson became that connecting link, and in late 1965 he made a mess of it. We turn now from the machinery that the Democrats created to the way their economic policies were carried out.

The
Tarnished
Miracle

What went wrong with the American economy between 1965 and 1968?

The early reflationary moves of the Kennedy administration had to be undertaken almost by stealth, because the conservative coalition in Congress (and allegedly the foreign gnomes waiting to run from the dollar) would not have approved of them. However by admirable sleight of hand, the fiscal dividend was overspent in 1961–62 by increases in social security and other spending, plus in 1962 an investment tax credit on purchases of machinery and equipment (which was a tax cut that went to businessmen, so that some conservative congressmen regarded it as respectable).

The key point of the Kennedy strategy was a sizeable cut in income tax rates in 1963, but Congress delayed this (and Walter Heller got into a row for complaining about America's "puritan ethic"). After Kennedy's assassination, the cut was granted to President Johnson, almost as an act of penance, in 1964. Of it the CEA was to say:

This tax cut was unprecedented in many respects. When fully effective in 1965, it added more than $11 billion to private purchasing power—the largest stimulative action ever undertaken in peacetime. It was enacted while the federal budget was in deficit and while expenditures were rising. It was designed explicitly to sustain and invigorate expansion up to potential output rather than to combat an existing or imminent recession. This major action was followed by the enactment of a phased reduction in excise taxes in the spring of 1965.

The tragedy was that all this was put into effect just before it was beginning not to be needed.

46   The original strategy for 1965 onwards was to devote virtually the whole of the fiscal dividend to the "war on poverty," by which President Johnson hoped to tackle the problem of Negro misery at its roots. In the later months of 1965, however, Secretary of Defence McNamara and Secretary of State Rusk impressed on the President that they would need to spend a lot more money on the war in Vietnam as well. They did not pass their views on immediately to the economic decision-makers, with whom—under the strange American cabinet system—they anyway rarely met.

When the troika heard what was happening, they recommended in early 1966 that President Johnson should ask Congress for a tax increase. The President was reluctant for three reasons. First, he was afraid that Congress would then cut back on his funds for his war on poverty. Secondly, he did not want to stimulate a new debate in Congress on Vietnam at that time. Thirdly, he said that Congress would not pass a tax increase anyway, especially as 1966 was a congressional election year. Some of the economic advisers, having just emerged from a battle with a Congress that had been unwilling to cut taxes, plainly found this last statement difficult to believe.

The troika's proudest trophy was that the great expansion had been carried out until then with barely any price inflation. With government expenditure rising, and thereby destroying the full employment budget surplus just as full employment was in fact attained, they feared that inflation would now start in earnest. The fear was made a certainty when the wage-price guideposts broke down in the airline mechanics' dispute. President Kennedy had kept in operation one of the most efficient and effective incomes policies that the world has seen. Mrs Castle ought to read about it some time. It was based on anti-monopoly policies against both the labour and business sectors. The President persuaded trade unions not to press for centrally bargained wage increases above the level of the average rise in productivity, and had promised in return that monopolistically determined prices would not be raised unreasonably (when the steel unions in 1962 kept down their wage settlement, and the steel companies promptly announced an increase in prices, Kennedy mobilised the force of public opinion to make the steel companies rescind their intention). But

47

profits in the expanding and capital-intensive airlines were protected by restraints against competition by the world air fares cartel; the airline mechanics pointed to risen profits, went on strike, won an inflationary increase from the airlines who thought they were thereby buying off trouble (but were in fact, of course, making themselves even more favourite targets for union pressure from that day on), and it was widely advertised that income guidelines had broken down.

The credit crunch

The authorities tried to hold the line with a stern monetary policy instead. This was the famous "credit crunch" of 1966, when the squeeze on money supply forced American banks to bring back to New York every dollar they could (incidentally, helping to precipitate the sterling crisis of July, 1966, in the process). It is usual to say that monetary policy cannot work when financial policy is pulling against it. It is therefore worth pointing out that in 1966 in America it did. The rate of increase of final demand was slowed dramatically; admittedly, far too much of the burden fell on the construction industry (housing starts halved in nine months), but consumption flagged too. Because production temporarily went on rising while demand slackened, inventories piled up; and the inventory recession in the first quarter of 1967 led to

48

a small drop in GNP, although only for those three months.

Meanwhile, however, expenditure on the war in Vietnam was due to go on rising. The chosen strategy for 1967 was to ease monetary policy during the first and recession-hit half of the year, but to increase taxes after the middle of the year. At this stage, the blow fell. President Johnson's forebodings in early 1966 proved right after all. Congress was just as unwilling to raise taxes as it had previously been to lower them; it was not until the summer of 1968 that the increase was agreed to. And this delay threatened to have a dangerous effect on the mood and trends of economic policy as Richard Nixon came to power.

49

What the voters called inflation

On the hustings during the 1968 presidential election campaign, politicians did not find the voters to be particularly grateful to the Democrats for the economic expansion of the 1960s. The reason was fairly simple. It is true that, on any long-sighted view, the great expansion since 1961 had gone forward smoothly. America had got used to an annual growth rate of around or over 4 per cent. At present levels of GNP (1969's GNP is likely to be some $930 billion), this means real expansion at an annual rate of between $35 billion and $40 billion, or a quarterly rate of around $9 billion (say, a steady quarterly increase in money GNP of around $13 billion or $14 billion, if price inflation were no more than about 2 per cent per annum).

The trouble was that between 1965 and 1968 the greater part of the rise in GNP was absorbed by: (a) rising expenditures on the Vietnam war; (b) the government's spending on social welfare. There would have been more gravy available if real expansion had proceeded at a steady $35 billion to $40 billion annual rate, but the credit crunch in 1966 meant that about six months' worth of annual expansion was lost. It followed that consumption by the ordinary worker had to be held back. It was held back. This can be shown by statistics for the "average spendable weekly earnings of a worker in manufacturing industry with three dependents, in terms of fixed (1957–59) prices"; this is a mouthful of typically American statistical jargon, but if you read it through twice you will see what it means.

These average real weekly earnings had risen from $77.70 in 1960 to $88.06 in 1965; thereafter they actually declined below the $88 mark in 1966 and 1967, and rose only to $88.51 by election day in November, 1968. Most of this slowdown in real earnings was caused by the greater pace of price inflation. Between 1965 and election day, when the real earnings of the aforementioned "average" worker in manufacturing were rising by only 45 cents a week, his money earnings rose by $12.44 a week, from $96.78 to $109.22.

50

Republican politicians on the hustings in 1968 naturally found blue-collar workers indignant at the standstill in real earnings. They would have been indignant however it had been brought about, but the battle cry was understandably against inflation. This was music to the ears of some Republican businessmen, who equate inflation with sin. There therefore seemed to be a danger, as the Nixon team rolled back towards power, that the Republicans would fight a battle against the working man's variant of the complaint against inflation (by which he meant the stopping of a rise in his real earnings) through a conservative-type of anti-inflation policy (i.e., by retarding the rate of growth of real production, and thus of the only means of putting real earnings up).

51

Impact of 1968

This danger was compounded by another misfortune in mid-1968. Up until that time, the official economists' forecasts of variations in the rate of growth had been generally accurate. They had slightly underestimated the strength of the 1965–66 boom (chiefly because their own government had not told them how much it was preparing to spend in Vietnam), and possibly underestimated the slowdown in early 1967 (which was aided by a growth in the personal savings rate that—Chicago school "monetary economists" aver—usually does follow a period of money squeeze, although some Keynesian economists deny this). But there had been no major mistake. The first real blooper came last summer, when Congress at last agreed to President Johnson's request for a tax increase, and perversely added an obligatory cut in government expenditure to it.

At this time, some people feared an overkill. The Federal Reserve therefore loosened monetary policy, over the protest of its most conservative members—such as the now very right-wing Federal Reserve Bank of New York, which said that inflation continued to be the main problem. Unfortunately, the conservatives in mid-1968 proved to be right, for one or more of the following reasons:

(1) Equations for forward estimates of businessmen's fixed investment traditionally take into account such factors as the utilisation rate of existing capacity (which in mid-1968 was not particularly high), the anticipated state of corporate liquidity, and businessmen's estimates of the level of demand immediately ahead. But these equations were drawn up in a period when businessmen expected intermittent recessions. The long expansion during the sixties may have removed this assumption. Business investment plans after the tax increase therefore remained almost unbelievably buoyant.

(2) There is increasing evidence—one returns here to the arguments of the Chicago University economists—that a tax increase may not work as either a lasting or a prompt curb upon demand unless monetary policy (and particularly control of the money supply) is working in the same direction. This is despite the fact that America's

experience in 1966 also suggests that monetary policy on its own can act as a surprisingly effective damper, even if fiscal policy is not running in harness with it.

(3) Some people say that the cut in consumer spending forecast after the tax increase last summer has merely been postponed.

It will become apparent from a later chapter that I am inclined to give more credence to the second of these arguments than many other economists outside Chicago University do. But the second half of 1968 was a deplorable time to test the theory out. More power has thereby been given to the elbow of those conservative members of the Federal Reserve of New York and others who (in the expressive American phrase) were anyway already "loaded for bear." This happened at a time when the Nixon administration was coming to office, believing that the worst thing that had happened in the past two years was a recrudescence of price inflation (which, as measured by the consumer price index, was 2.8 per cent in 1967, 4.2 per cent in 1968, and at an annual rate of 5 per cent by the last quarter of 1968). As I flew to Washington last February, I was afraid that I might find the new administration to be loaded for bear also. What I found instead was a moderately—but only moderately —pleasant surprise.

53

What
Is
the
Republican
Way?

A guide to the preoccupations of Professor Burns, and to the policies of Professor McCracken.

54   When the Republican administration swarmed into office last January, there was lively speculation on how the real power of economic decision-making would in practice divide between the members of the new team. This speculation was still continuing in early March, not least among the members of the new team themselves.

One early theory had been that the power of the troika might be weakened by subjection to the rule of either the "lone ranger" or else of what was rather widely called "that silly new cabinet committee." The lone ranger is Arthur Burns, a professor of economics well known for his studies of the trade cycle, and a personal friend of President Nixon's, who is installed in the White House as what he himself has called "a sort of minister without portfolio."

But a visit to Arthur Burns suggests strongly that macro-economic policy is just about the only thing he is not busying himself with at the moment. He is the co-ordinator of much of the intended domestic legislative programme; and the man through whom other staff members in the White House work to the President, if they want to get action on a lot of individual subjects—such as policy for the exploding universities, or securing the funding of some particular pet programme (but "show that it can be done economically, and set out the case on one piece of paper, please"), or whatever. Trade cycle policy, and arguments about general management of demand, are things that Professor Burns is temperamentally inclined to believe should be left to people with time for a lot of delving into the figures; and time is a commodity that he no longer has. He will be a force with considerable influence on social policy, and in a conservative direction; he is no lover of the welfare state. But the decision to go for boom or slump is not one that will pass, on a single sheet of paper, across that busy desk.

A troika of old friends

I am less certain about the impact of President Nixon's new cabinet committee on economic policy. The troika have been joined on this committee by President Nixon, Vice President Agnew, Arthur Burns, and the Secretaries of Commerce, Labour, and Agriculture. One Democrat's story in alleged explanation of its creation is that the Secretary of Commerce, Mr Stans, had at one time been promised membership of the troika, and that this new committee (and the pretence that it is a key organisation) is a device for wasting the time of a lot of other busy people in order to save Mr Stans's face. A more loyal explanation, given by an adulator of President Nixon's, is "the troika is still the body that will make the main policy recommendations, but under the old system those other guys whose interests were affected could only come to the President to complain. Now they will all be sitting round the table together, and this will hopefully economise on the President's time." John Kennedy had some such occasional cabinet committees, such as his cabinet committee on economic growth in 1962, generally to rubber-stamp decisions the troika had made. One's hope is that the new overlarge cabinet committee will just do the same; but it is important that it should not sprout equally overlarge sub-committees of civil servants below it.

56

A peculiarity of the new troika is that all three members are long-time personal friends of one another. They are (a) Secretary of the Treasury David Kennedy, a gentle Mormon banker who is universally described as "a good delegator"; (b) Director of the Bureau of the Budget Robert Mayo, who used once to be the chief executive in the Chicago bank of which Secretary Kennedy was president, and thus the man whom Secretary Kennedy was used to delegating to; (c) Chairman of the Council of Economic Advisers Paul McCracken, an extremely competent professor of economics from the University of Michigan, and therefore also no stranger to the Chicago business community. All have also had the experience of working in or for government before, though at lower levels than their new eminence.

Robert Mayo is an accountancy-minded efficiency expert, who in March was working from barbarously early hours in the morning at ways of trimming the expenditure of the American government, which he likes to call "the largest financial undertaking in the world." If ever the requirement became to reflate the economy, he presumes that somebody would tell him; but at the moment saving something bigger than candle-ends is his more than full-time job. My guess is that this attitude, plus Secretary Kennedy's belief in delegation, will leave Paul McCracken as the most important arbiter of domestic economic policy within the troika, and thus within the Nixon administration, for some time to come.

The McCracken doctrine

The first thing to say about Paul McCracken is that he is a very undoctrinaire man; he enters an entirely sensible qualification against almost every opinion he expresses. Having said that, he has a distinctive view about the proper role of economic policy, and this view now becomes important for the world. Although I am leaving

WHAT IS THE REPUBLICAN WAY?

out too many of the qualifications, a reasonably fair
summary probably runs as follows:

(1) Mr McCracken believes that the normal equilib-
rium annual rate of growth in real GNP for the United
States in most of the next five or ten years should be
around 4 per cent. The calculation here is: America can
count at present upon an annual growth of just under
2 per cent in the labour force, plus around an annual 3
per cent productivity growth in the private sector, but it
must subtract slightly from this 5 per cent because of
the expectation of lower productivity growth in the
public sector and because of a probable slight fall in the
length of the working week.

(2) He is inclined to believe that the United States
would usually achieve somewhere around this 4 per cent
annual real growth, plus somewhere around 2 per cent of
annual price inflation, if the country (a) expanded the
money supply at about 6 per cent per annum; and (b)
fixed the budget at a point where it would just about
balance at the point of full employment.

(3) Basing himself on these assumptions, Mr Mc-
Cracken is opposed to following stop-go or zig-zag or
"fine-tuning" policies. He is clearly not enamoured of the
type of economic policy-maker who reacts to temporarily
inflationary indicators in the quarter just past by impos-
ing emergency fiscal measures that will take real effect
only in six months' time, by when it is highly possible that
a restimulation is what would really be required. But he
agrees that there are some circumstances in which an

58

activist policy is required. If underproduction lasted for a longer period than is needed for mere inventory adjustment, he would ease monetary or fiscal policy; and if unacceptable inflation has set in, he would tighten it.

(4) Mr McCracken plainly believes that an unacceptable inflation has set in, with last year's rise in prices at an annual rate of around 5 per cent by the December quarter. He is therefore in favour of following a tight money policy this year, but is by no means hawkish in this respect. Although he mentioned no figures, I got the impression that 3 per cent real growth and 3 per cent price inflation in 1969 would be regarded as a movement on target—although Mr McCracken would probably then still want to keep a fairly tight money policy for 1970 so that price inflation would moderate some more then (although he would hope that the real growth rate wouldn't) .

Some people of importance in the United States would be ready to see real growth pushed considerably lower than 3 per cent, in order to "kill the inflationary germ" about which some people (for example, at the Federal Reserve Bank of New York) sound pretty hawkish. Mr McCracken is a dove for two reasons. First, he does not want to push up unemployment too far; he fully recognises what effect such a rise could have among Negroes.

Secondly, he is an internationalist, and believes that the recent sharp rise in American imports has been largely a function of rising money national income. While all Americans certainly hope that the United States will not

59

repeat the 23 per cent rise in imports that it marked up in 1968, liberals in the Nixon administration realise that world trade could become caught in a real deflationary crisis if the growth of American imports dropped for long far below the 7 to 9 per cent annual rate which most economists there tend to associate with a 6 per cent annual rise in money GNP. If the rise in money GNP ever dropped to 3½ per cent—say, 1¾ per cent real growth and 1¾ per cent price rise—then some econometricians believe that the growth in American imports that year would be nil. "And in that event," says one economist in the White House's executive office building, "you Europeans who are telling us to put our balance of payments in order would fairly quickly change your tune." We would indeed.

60

But who runs money?

The next question, however, is: how do Mr McCracken and Secretary Kennedy and Mr Mayo and their colleagues expect to enforce the moderately restrictive policy which is their (and President Nixon's) chosen recipe for this year? I made my tour round the corridors of power before the continuingly buoyant economic indicators in the first quarter of the year induced President Nixon to toughen his stance of policy, and send a message to Congress announcing that he was calling for an increased budget surplus of $5.8 billion in the fiscal year up to July,

1970; and before the wide advertisement that this would be the largest budget surplus since 1951. But the point is, of course, that the Nixon administration is aiming at this surplus at a time when America is in very full employment. For reasons that will appear in the last three chapters of the survey, it is a rather larger budget surplus than I believe to be socially desirable. However, it is a surplus that will still amount to only just over half of 1 per cent of GNP, at a time when unemployment is down at 3.4 per cent and inflation is presently between 4 and 5 per cent per annum. I do not regard this sort of budgeting as inconsistent with Mr McCracken's policy of keeping the budget fairly neutral in conditions of full (as distinct from inflationarily overfull) employment.

It follows that the main weapon for any actual disinfla-   61
tion in 1969 is likely to be control of the money supply. But—and here is the remarkable rub—management of monetary policy rests with the Federal Reserve, some of whose mandarins do not believe very firmly in control of the money supply, and a few of whom would even like to prove that management of the money supply doesn't work at all. We have come to the most intriguing economic squabble in America today: a squabble in which men at the Federal Reserve for a time last year seemed willing to send their economy along the path of some inflation (which they don't want to follow, although I happen rather to want them to), largely because they wished to persuade themselves that their most upbraiding and nominally most conservative critic is wrong (al-

though I, as what they would call an inflationist, actually believe that he is largely right). We have come, in short, to the battle between the irritated bankers of Washington and New York and the maddening gnome of Chicago. See, see, I have been visiting both the Federal Reserve and Professor Milton Friedman.

62

Friedman
Versus
the
Fed

The debate over money supply.

At intervals of approximately three weeks the open market committee of the Federal Reserve System meets in solemn conclave, in order to decide the course of America's monetary policy—and thus, under present circumstances, of America's domestic economic policy—until its next meeting. Those attending the committee are the seven governors of the Federal Reserve Board at Washington, and the presidents of the twelve district Federal Reserve banks (although, under an antiquated rule, only five of the latter, elected in rotation, are allowed to vote). The subject on which they are voting is the instruction to be given to Mr Alan Holmes, the "manager of the account" in New York, about the guidelines he should follow when deciding whether to buy or sell government securities, and thus whether to expand or contract America's money supply, over the next three weeks. The terms of this instruction are nowadays fixed with one eye on the condition of the economy, and the other eye on a ridiculous semantic paddy.

The monetary school of economists at the University of Chicago, led by Professor Milton Friedman, has long proclaimed that the object of monetary policy should simply be to keep the money supply expanding at a fairly steady pace. The fashionable figures to argue for now are a rate of expansion of some definition of currency plus bank deposits of between 5 and 7 per cent per annum; the favoured rate used to be lower before people realised how swiftly the American economy can grow. The guts of the argument between Dr Friedman and at least some at the Fed used to be whether the level of money supply had any direct importance at all. It is fair comment that most reputable economists now accept at least part of Friedman's statistical proof that to some extent it does: changes in money supply do affect total demand after a varying time lag, which Friedman thinks averages around six months under present American conditions. The argument has now shifted to whether the Fed's hands would be "too rigidly tied" if it were given a quantitative rule for money supply.

It is important to realise that some economists who have been trained under the influence of Chicago—and they include more than a roomful now working for the Nixon administration—think that some tying of the Fed's hands is precisely what is needed. "At present," says one (who has to be nameless),

America's economic policy is set by these nineteen guys who come together every three weeks to draft a

specific directive, which it is impossible for nineteen
guys sitting together to do, so they say something like
"let's keep things going the way that they have been
going, although we are at present rather uncertain
what that way is."

The Federal Reserve indignantly denies this caricature,
but records of these directives to Mr Holmes are now
published three months later in the *Federal Reserve
Bulletin*. At the time I was in Washington the latest
(January) issue of the *Bulletin* showed that the directive
after the meeting of the open market committee on October 8th began with a fairly general account of economic
conditions, and then went on:

65

> In this situation, it is the policy of the Federal Open
> Market Committee to foster financial conditions con-
> ducive to sustainable economic growth, continued re-
> sistance to inflationary pressures, and attainment of
> reasonable equilibrium in the country's balance of
> payments.

> To implement this policy, system open market opera-
> tions, until the next meeting of the committee, should
> be conducted with a view to maintaining about the
> prevailing conditions in money and short-term credit
> markets; provided, however, that operations shall be
> modified, to the extent permitted by the forthcoming
> Treasury refunding operation, if bank credit expan-

sion appears to be significantly exceeding current projections.

Um!

Translated from the nothingness

The economists at the Federal Reserve, of course, have a sophisticated answer to that cry of "Um!" They argue that the directives to the manager of the account are more meaningful than the published jargon may make them appear. When the manager is told to "maintain about the prevailing conditions in money and short-term credit markets," he knows that he has to try to keep approximate stability in:

(a) The cost of overnight money;
(b) the cost of three months' money; and
(c) the level of commercial banks' net free reserves.

When he is told to squeeze on these variables, as he has been told since October, commercial banks will be likely to have to come to borrow at the discount window from the Federal Reserve. Once they are borrowing there, the Fed can call the tune, telling the commercial banks at what speed they must run down their commercial lending.

However, it is recognised that the commercial banks can sometimes temporarily thwart the Fed's clutches.

66

For example they are able to draw in Euro-dollars from abroad during a squeeze, although this becomes unprofitable as soon as Euro-dollar interest rates go close to market interest rates for new bank lending in America; and they were able to draw in funds on certificates of deposit until market interest rates on securities competitive with such certificates went above the ceiling that the Fed's Regulation Q allows the commercial banks to pay for such funds. Accordingly, the Fed's manager is nowadays given an additional guideline. He is told, within a range, what approximate growth rate for one definition of the money supply is expected to result if he follows his instructions about how he should seek to affect factors (a), (b), and (c) above. If the money supply moves outside the projected limits, he is encouraged to operate in the open market in order to try to get it back within them. At the end of last year, the behind-the-scenes instruction was in fact something like: "if money supply is rising by more than 4 per cent per annum, sell government securities."

The definition of the money supply used is the so-called "credit proxy," which is the sum of the deposit liabilities of member banks subject to reserve requirements. This differs fairly notably from Dr Friedman's definition of money supply M_1 (which equals currency plus demand deposits); and it differs somewhat even from his definition M_2 (which equals currency plus private deposits) because the credit proxy excludes notes and coin, but includes government bank deposits. But the Fed's spokesmen say that the credit proxy is the only figure for money supply which is easily available on a day-to-day basis, and that it includes slightly less "noise" than other estimates of money supply (i.e., is less hit by wholly irregular movements and shifting seasonal factors). Moreover, raising their voice by several octaves—for this has become one of those not infrequent economic arguments where staid men are clearly getting cross with one another—they add that Dr Friedman is always changing his definitions of money supply, not only as between M_1 and M_2, but in other more complicated ways as well, so that it is not surprising that movements in money GNP can be made to correlate, after some time lag, with one or other of them.

68

Chicago doctrine

Over, therefore, to see Milton Friedman himself: a vivacious sparrow of a man, who holds sway at the University of Chicago. Friedman's forte seems to me to be economic conversation, at which he is immensely impressive: more impressive, really, than in his writings, in which one is never quite sure whether in any particular sentence he is playing the conservative, the iconoclast, the mathematician, the historian, the philosopher, or the imp. He is also, incidentally, far far less reactionary than his reputation—for example, as Senator Goldwater's economic adviser in the 1964 election campaign—has led many people on this side of the Atlantic to proclaim.

His primary reply to the Federal Reserve is that it is impossible for its unfortunate manager of the account (a) to try to aim at certain conditions for short-term interest rates and for commercial banks' net free reserves, while (b) trying to control the money supply—because that is often equivalent to instructing the poor fellow to ride two horses in diametrically different directions at once.

At any one time, according to Dr Friedman, various outside factors are necessarily working through the market to alter interest rates. For much of last year, for example, the dominant factor was an increase in the rate of inflation, serving to press interest rates up. But when this happens, the manager of the Fed's account, following his orders from the open market committee, is apt to decide that the pressure is no doubt a temporary aberration, which requires to be ironed out. He therefore "leans against" the rise in interest rates by buying securities. When he does this, he increases the money supply, stokes up inflation, and then finds that interest rates are going up again. He therefore leans against them some more—until the process has stoked up inflation so far that everybody calls for a change in policy which will bring money supply under control.

Unfortunately, at this stage, the situation could become more dangerous still: especially if money supply is brought under too tight a control, pushing the economy towards recession. In this case, the underlying market

69

trend will be for interest rates to fall. But the Federal Reserve, still fighting the last battle, may then still be ordering its manager to lean against any such "premature" reduction in interest rates. It could thereby turn an incipient slowdown into something more serious.

As for the other main order at present given to the manager of the account—that he should look to the level of the commercial banks' net free reserves—the Chicago school argues that this is often irrelevant. What matters is not the absolute level of those reserves, but their relationship to the level of reserves that the banks want to hold. If the Federal Reserve's discount rate is low and the profit turn for commercial lending relatively high, then banks might temporarily be very willing to have low reserves and go to borrow at the Fed's discount window.

It is tempting to follow this argument for several pages more, but I expect I will be writing at more length on central banking policy in *The Economist* on several occasions in future; I had better merely say in this survey that I find the main part of Dr Friedman's criticism— although not all of the regression equations of some of his followers—to be convincing. I think that the ground rules given out by the Federal Reserve open market committee are misleading ones, and that they do lead the Federal Reserve (like other central banks) too often to lean against the natural trend of interest rates. As the Federal Reserve is at present squeezing quite hard in the money markets, it is possible that before the end of 1969 the natural trend will be for interest rates to drop, because the American economy is being pushed towards slowdown or recession. There is a danger that the Federal Reserve, still talking about the need to curb inflation once and for all, might then lean against this, and risk causing something worse. But the greatest comfort I have got from my visit to Washington is a belief that the Nixon administration has enough wide-awake economists not really to allow this to happen on a world-shattering scale. Unfortunately, it may just allow it to happen on a ghetto-exploding scale instead. And so we return, in the last three chapters of this survey, to America's most mortal internal danger.

71

The
Last
Migration

The number of angry young black men in America's cities is due to increase spectacularly over the next five years. The framers of America's economic policies should never forget this.

Anything written about the urban crisis in the United States is bound to be controversial, and these last three chapters in this survey will be no exception. What is not controversial is that America is now experiencing the aftermath of the latest of the many mass immigrations that have been the main feature, and furnished the principal dynamic, of its social history. The last immigration has been from within, and it has been black.

The huge fall in farm population which recent decades of agricultural mechanisation have made possible in all industrial countries—in America the percentage of workers on the land has dropped from 25 in 1935 to 5 now—has naturally had a particular effect on what is politely called the formerly labour-intensive agriculture of the south-eastern United States. The great-great-grandsons of the slaves have been marching north. In

1910, some 91 per cent of the nation's 9.8 million Negroes still lived in the south, mostly in the countryside. By 1966, some 69 per cent of America's 22.5 million Negroes lived in the cities, increasingly in the north. In the 1940s and 1950s net Negro migration from the south averaged 150,000 a year, and in the first half of the 1960s it was still close to 100,000 a year. It has slowed dramatically only in the last three years, as the newspaper headlines have shouted aloud how frightening the conditions in the urban ghettos now are.

Flaming youth in smouldering ghettos

This recent slowing has not stopped the growth of Negro population in the cities. The reason is that the birth rate has now taken over from migration as the big expansionary factor, and this is responsible for a main characteristic of today's ghettos: namely, that they are swarming with young people. More than half of black Americans today are below the age of 22. In part, this is because of the fall in black infant mortality in recent years (although the rate is still wickedly higher than that for white Americans). In part, it is because the birth rate among black Americans is still typical of an underdeveloped country; poor black women have much larger than average families, while university-educated black women actually have fewer children than their white graduate sisters.

But another complicating factor in some cities is America's crazily decentralised welfare system. Under it, the size of welfare payments depends on the relative liberality of the state governments, so that it is not surprising that in 1965 maximum payments to a completely destitute mother with three children ranged from a starvation dole of $50 a month in Mississippi to a tolerably generous $246 a month in New York. Moreover, barriers are still imposed against welfare payments to families who have potential male breadwinners in the house, even if they are not managing to get decently paid jobs. The result has been a sizeable migration of husbandless black women with large families from the cruel south to the less brutal cities of the north, and also a clear indication to any poorly paid Negro that the best way he can get welfare benefits for his children and their mother is to desert them and disappear. Partly because of this, and partly because matriarch-ruled families are more common in the Negro community anyway, a full ┼ 30 per cent of black families in the big cities last year had women as their heads.

It is important to be clear what this means. It is a statistical and sociological fact that the commonest committers of violent street crimes are young men between the ages of 16 and 24. In 1966 over 70 per cent of America's robberies, burglaries, and rapes were committed by men under 25. The statistics also show that a youth is particularly liable to become delinquent if he is living in dilapidated housing near the centre of a big

74

metropolitan area, without a father in the house, with low income, unstable employment, little education, and in a culture that has a grievance against society and its police. The United States has now managed to create exactly these conditions in most of its big cities with over 1 million population. As immigration into the black ghettos has continued, and whites have moved out to the suburbs, the percentage of the population of such cities that is Negro has grown from 13 to 26 per cent between 1950 and 1966.

Moreover, the age structure in the ghettos is not going to get better. In the immediate future it is going to get much worse. Last year's Kerner report estimated that between 1966 and 1975 the number of young Negroes in the ghettos aged from 15 to 24 will rise by 1.6 million, or 40.1 per cent. The Kerner report went on: 75

> This group has the highest unemployment rate in the nation, commits a relatively high proportion of all crimes, and plays the most significant role in civil disorders. By the same token, it is a great reservoir of underused human resources. . . .

Probably nothing can be done to prevent a rise in violence in the cities in the early 1970s, under circumstances where those most liable to be violent will be increasing at this rate. To my mind it follows with blazing obviousness that the first priority of economic policy in those early 1970s, *pace* Mr Nixon and the Federal Reserve,

really is not going to be to "curb inflation." It is going
to be to see that more of these young people get jobs—
and ones that will mean they can bring up the next tidal
wave, of their own children, far from the ghettos of
today.

The war on poverty is easy

Note that emphasis on getting jobs and going suburban.
It is a misconception to suppose that the key economic
problem for black Americans today is poverty. The key
problems are the need for dispersion and the worrying
underemployment of young members of the black
underclass. By contrast, the war on black poverty should
be dead easy to win. That will sound controversial, but
fainthearts should look at the figures of incomes—and
how they have been changing in recent years.

In 1966, some 28 per cent of the 5 million black
American families had incomes of over $7,000 a year,
and thus enjoyed a middle class or upper class standard
of living by any other nation's standards, and a median
standard of living by America's own; the proportion of
black American families above this real income level has
doubled since 1960. Another 41 per cent of black
families had incomes between $3,000 and $7,000 a year;
this left them disadvantaged compared with the average
white American, but their standards of consumption (as
distinct from their environmental jungle) are on a par

with those of working class west Europeans. There remains, it is true, the bottom third of non-white families —often the larger ones, containing in 1967 8.3 million people, or 35.3 per cent of black Americans (plus other non-whites, such as American Indians and Eskimos) — who were below the official American definition of the poverty line. In 1966, some 17.6 million white Americans (usually older ones) were also below this poverty line, and they represented 10.2 per cent of the white community.

But two qualifying points should be made straightway. First, America draws its poverty line at levels that would be considered generous abroad.* Amid all the sad statistics poured forth about the ghettos, it is worth remembering that in 1967 some 88 per cent of black American families had television sets. The poverty line in America is defined by saying that nobody can be expected to spend more than about a third of his income on food, and then studying the cost of a nutritionally adequate diet of the sort of food that the poor actually eat ("they don't eat grits, they do eat hamburgers, so it's hamburgers that

77

* It is always difficult to say at what exchange rate relative standards of living should be compared. Obviously, life in America is more expensive than would be shown to an Englishman by straight conversion at $2.40 to the £1; but a distinction should be made between America's much higher prices for services (which hit visiting moguls in the hotels very hard, luckily for local salaries of staff on the spot) and its competitive prices for many goods. Some international organisations have been using $3.43 to the £1 when remunerating overseas employees, and some British businesses with staff in America have been using $5; but these figures make allowance for the fact that a family that would have a middle class standard of living in one country is not expected to scrape by at a labourer's standard in another country, even if in that new country the labourers are better off.

are in," says one official) . The result is a calculation that a four-person non-farm family is poor if its annual income is less than $3,335 at 1966 prices of consumer goods, with adjustments made for people who do not happen to belong to four-person non-farm families in fairly obvious proportions.

The second—and even more striking—point is that by 1967 a transfer of only $9.7 billion a year to the poor would have been needed to lift every American above this generously defined poverty line. This amounts to only about a quarter of a single year's normal increase in real GNP. It is rather less than the yield of the 1968 surcharge on income tax—the special tax increase made by President Johnson last year—which Mr Nixon has recommended should be halved after January 1st next.

Moreover, the war on poverty is not only easy to win. It has been in process of being won during this last decade. The last report of the Democrats' CEA was able to say with justice:

> If the 1961–68 reductions in the number of poor persons could be continued, poverty would be eliminated entirely in about ten years. If the record of 1968 could be continued, poverty would be eliminated in about 5½ years.

It is true that a general rise in prosperity will not be enough to keep up this rate of progress. This is because 59 per cent of poor families are now headed by either

women with children, or the disabled, or the elderly—
and most of these will need help through some reform
of the social services, such as by advance to a negative
income tax (see page 104). But with under $10 billion
a year needed to close the entire poverty gap, this reform
really is not beyond America's grasp. It is also required
by America's conscience. Although the general figures
of the war on poverty are comforting, there still remain
in this richest country of the world—particularly among
the rural Negro poor in the south—some pockets of
dreadful malnutrition, which only occasionally emerge
into the headlines and manage to shock the nation.

Schools and housing   79

The other great need of the social services, apart from
income maintenance, is to aid the dispersion of the
Negro population. This is the only way to solve educational, housing, and environmental problems in the sad
cities.

On the face of the educational figures, the flaming
youths of the black ghettos are not untutored young
men. Some 83 per cent of black Americans aged 16 and
17 are still at school (compared with 89 per cent of white
Americans of that age), and the proportion of black
Americans going on to university is higher than is usual
among young people in Europe. The trouble is that the
quality of education at the bottom is appallingly low. In

his chapter in the Brookings report, *Agenda for the Nation*, Mr Ralph Tyler reports:

> According to the best estimates that can be made . . .
> approximately one-fifth of the children of the United
> States do not attain the level of literacy required for
> available employment; a similar number may not gain
> the understanding needed for citizenship and satisfy-
> ing personal lives. In rural and urban slum areas 40
> to 60 per cent of the children in the sixth grade per-
> form at second grade level or below on achievement
> tests. The educationally deprived are heavily concen-
> trated among the poor, Negroes, Mexican Americans,
> Puerto Ricans, and American Indians.

80 Mr Tyler is emeritus director of the Centre for Advanced Study in the Behavioural Sciences at Stanford, and one suspects that his assessment of the level of literacy any civilised man requires suffers a bit from the American meritocrat's habitual tendency to overrate the modern world. But the point is inescapable that the *de facto* all-black schools in the ghettos have been overwhelmed by the tidal wave of children in these areas, and are today as unsatisfactory as the old *de jure* all-black schools in the south from which these children's mothers came. Moreover, it is not going to be possible under present conditions to attract enough good teachers down into the ghetto schools, however much money is spent. The solution must be to spread many more of the next gen-

eration of black schoolchildren round the schools of suburbia, where their families must also go.

The housing of about one-fifth of the inhabitants of Negro ghettos must be called appalling slums by any standard, and the housing of another two-fifths is called inadequate by American standards. Environmental services—such as the collection of refuse—are generally foul. But some of the areas hit by the worst troubles are not slums: for example, the Los Angeles Negro district of Watts, which erupted in a bad riot (34 people killed) in 1965. That is why one doubts whether even extensive rebuilding and other improvements in model cities' proposed "model neighbourhoods"—in which it is proposed to pull together all existing federal programmes for the poor—will necessarily reach the root of the environmental problem.

81

The root problem is that Negro areas of American cities have what is called a "separation index" of 86 per cent. This means that 86 per cent of the Negroes in them would have to move in order to have black and white intermingled evenly across the cities and commuterdom. This requirement is not as impossible of reasonably early solution as it may sound. An astonishing 20 per cent of white Americans in urban and suburban areas move house each year—and remember that this white community is nine times larger than the Negro one. If there were a dropping of discriminatory practices against Negro purchases of houses in "white areas"—practices which are illegal, but by estate agents are flagrantly allowed—the "separation index" could be diluted quite quickly. Plenty of houses to dilute it come annually onto the market, and a steadily wealthier Negro community ought increasingly to be able to afford them. The material and moral incentive to move out of those horrible ghettos—into a suburbia where black faces are still a relative rarity—already exists. But there has got to be an effective banning of those discriminatory practices first.

Underemployment

82
The most urgent of all the problems in the ghettos, however, is the shortage of decent employment opportunities, especially for the young and dangerous. One of the most important points to keep shouting in the Nixon administration's ear is that economic growth still serves quite dramatically to mop up this unemployment, and that an economic slowdown is liable to cause a frightening new resurgence of waters behind the frail dam. Paul McCracken himself pointed out to Congress last February how

> important even a relatively small difference in the national average rate of unemployment may be for the disadvantaged. Between the fourth quarter of 1967 and the fourth quarter of 1968, when the seasonally un-

adjusted national average unemployment rate fell
from 3.7 to 3.2 per cent, the unemployment rate of
Negroes in urban poverty neighbourhoods of the 100
largest metropolitan areas fell from 9 to 6.4 per cent.

It is likely also to have had an impact on the rate of
underemployment in these areas, which is a bigger problem still.

In late 1966 the Department of Labour estimated that
the number of official defined unemployed in the ghettos
was probably outnumbered by two and a half to one by
those underemployed: defining the underemployed as
part-time workers looking vainly for full-time jobs, plus
full-time workers earning less than $3,000 a year, plus
people who have dropped hopelessly out of the labour
force. If this ratio still holds true today, then, even with
official unemployment down to 3.4 per cent in the nation
and to 6.4 per cent in the Negro ghettos, the total of
the sub-employed in those ghettos—i.e., unemployed and
underemployed together—may still be as high as 22½
per cent. That is the measure of the problem and of the
tragedy.

Moreover, this army of the underemployed is heavily
concentrated in the youngest and most disturbed age
groups. America's overall 3.2 per cent of recorded unemployment at the end of last year was made up of the
following extraordinarily differing ratios. For black teenagers the unemployment rate was a massive 21.5 per
cent; for white teenagers 11.6 per cent; for black women

83

5.9 per cent; for white women 3.2 per cent; for black adult men 3.4 per cent; for white adult men only 1.6 per cent. It is true that some of these huge teenage unemployment figures are bogus. America includes in its unemployment count kids still at school who are looking for out-of-school-hours, Saturday, or vacation jobs. But another part of the problem is that a 17-year-old looking for a full-time job in the United States tends to be regarded as a probably undesirable high school drop-out (remember that 83 per cent even of Negro 16- and 17-year-olds are still at school). And a still bigger problem is that racial discrimination in hiring is particularly bad for first jobs. The latest report from the President's Council of Economic Advisers had to note with just alarm that a "larger proportion of white male *drop-outs* aged 16 to 21 years of age secure skilled and semi-skilled jobs than non-white males who *graduate* from high school." Among small employers, at least, there is a danger that this discrimination may actually increase now that young Negroes of this age group have grown tougher and more militant in their image. The spread of that image has been one tragic consequence of the failure of the good-hearted sociological policies of the Johnson administration, to which the next chapter turns.

84

The Great Society's Shambles

Black Americans—like some white university presidents—have been given the cruellest of new crosses to bear. They are being subjected to minority mob rule within their own communities.

There is nothing the matter with Americans except their ideals. The real American is all right; it is the ideal American who is all wrong.   —G. K. Chesterton.

The more successful part of America's story in the 1960s needs to be written by economists and calculators, and to them should be allied all romantics. The unsuccessful part needs to be written by sociologists and psychiatrists, and from this part all romantics should be rigidly excluded. The tragedy is that in the "planning" of the sociological policies romantics were given full sway.

When President Johnson's Economic Opportunity Act was passed in 1964, it laid down that the anti-poverty programmes it initiated should be carried out with the "maximum feasible participation" of the poor residents of the communities concerned. In his book attacking this decision, called *Maximum Feasible Misunderstanding*, Mr Daniel Moynihan, now adviser on urban affairs to President Nixon, has rightly expostulated that the theory behind it was based on a strange (and essentially anti-democratic) insistence, which is very common among American liberals, that

> the "real" leaders of the people would not be the ostensible ones, that behind the institutional façade of political party committeemen, locality mayors, vice lords, and parish priests, there was to be found an echelon of uncorrupted men who, given opportunity, would assume leadership and . . . what? Change the world.

86

Since Mr Moynihan has been installed in the White House, there has been some attempt to explain that this book was particularly illustrative of the Irish in him; and Republicans have joined with Democrats to say that many community action programmes have done very good work (perhaps especially when they have annoyed Democratic mayors). But my dominant impression from this visit to America is that it was the most tragically deluded of errors—albeit made by the very nicest of people—in the United States of the mid-1960s thus federally to try to finance the calling up from the misty deep of supposed, but inevitably more militant than real, representatives of the Negro poor, and then set them to do battle against the power structure.

When the Economic Opportunity Act was conceived, the folk heroes of the liberals were boys' club leaders and others who had done good social work in the ghettos; the greatest glory would be, say, a Harlem resident, preferably (oh, heaven!) an ex-delinquent, who had given small groups of gang kids a new pride in themselves and their race. The vague idea was that the creation with federal funds of community action programmes in a thousand centres across the country would bring forth mass Negro participation under folk heroes of this type. This naturally did not happen. When elections were held among the poor to elect governing boards for these CAPs, the tiny turnouts were what every student of such elections should have expected: 0.7 per cent in Los Angeles, 2.4 per cent in Boston, 2.7 per cent in Philadelphia. One sort of progression on the boards was: first, control by middle class radicals; then a shift to control by black militants, voicing cries of revolution; then reaction from the larger white community, at which stage it would be discovered that corruption on some of the boards had been rife, and that some of the money had been used for purposes rather different from what the taxpayer had intended (in one case, allegedly, to buy telescopic sights for rifles).

It may be said that some of these sad failures should be treated as just bad jokes, and that they are outweighed by the many instances where CAPs have done brave work in particular fields under the direction of devoted social welfare professionals. But the rot has been helped to spread to two nasty developments.

A university experience

The less serious of these is the trouble in the universities. One of the earliest ugly battles was at Columbia University in New York, and I think Mr. Moynihan understates the case when he describes the origins thus:

88

> The elected [black] representatives of the Harlem community had several times ratified the construction by Columbia University of a gymnasium in Morningside Park. But the black students of the University decided that the assemblymen and senators, councilmen and borough presidents did not speak for the community, and that they did. This quickly enough becomes government, as one observer has noted, by a process of private nullification, which has never been especially good news for democracy. It would be absurd to blame the community action programmes of the war on poverty for this reductio ad absurdum, but the legitimation of something called "community control," in opposition to the established system of electoral representation, the assumption that established systems were somehow not meeting the needs of the people,

*was certainly much encouraged by the community
action movement.*

Obviously, there have been other causes of university
unrest: including many instances of old-fashioned university administration, and a very natural urge by the
majority of moderate students to come to the aid of any
of their extremist colleagues who are hit by flailing police
batons. But these conventional liberal excuses for what
had been happening are now out of date compared with
what is actually going on.

When I was in America in February and March, these
university disturbances were much in the news. I had an
opportunity to visit one when a major eastern university
held a seminar on South Africa, and invited me to attend   *89*
because of something I had written on that country in
The Economist last year. The grapevine said that there
was likely to be trouble at this seminar from black power
students and their hell-raising white brothers. Although
a lot of the invited participants at the seminar were active workers for an instant black South African revolution, others were wicked honkies like myself who were
doubtful of its immediate efficacy—and, anyway, there
had been some earlier trouble about the university allegedly putting some investment money into South
African shares. Amazingly, dreamy liberal intellectuals
in Washington still held some idealistic notions of what
a planned disturbance of this kind would be like. I was

told that I would find "the new left-wing spirit of American youth to be rather exciting."

What I found instead was the dreariest old Nazism. I am sorry if this contradicts accounts of America's new left by other British journalists—and I would dearly love to believe that one was witnessing here a new awakening to the desirability of actively reorganising society around new needs and ideals, including a much greater emphasis on justice and intellectual temerity and appreciation of beauty and gentleness—but I can only report on this one staged show that I saw. The cult of violence, the cult of youth, the cult of proclaiming that one was ruled by a plutocracy, the primordial enjoyment of a group togetherness in expressing hate, the raucous speeches made by proud leaders with practised (and, to those who do not remember the 1930s, impressive) timing and delivery—anybody over the age of 45 knows when and where in Europe youth was last asked to bathe in these emotions, and remembers grimly how many did so all too gladly.

As with Hitler's national socialists, the screamier orators present called themselves some sort of socialist, and used that proud term to absolve what they said from having any intellectual content whatsoever. There was a plain undercurrent of intimidation as youths roamed the classroom carrying buckets into which obviously non-revolutionary middle-aged gentlemen were requested to put entirely unaudited dollars, so as "to finance the South African revolution." Fortunately, I was not on the printed programme, and a kindly don agreed with me that, as things were turning out, I probably could not "constructively use my own experience." I most gratefully accepted this invitation to run scared, and was by now billing myself only as a foreign journalist asking earnest questions. Sample question to a white student member of the "rather exciting" radical intellectual group: "why do you think American troops are in Vietnam?" Answer: "because our big corporations want to steal the tin."

That evening the undercurrent of intimidation turned into an overcurrent. When we arrived in the main hall for a speech on South Africa by a prominent left-wing congressman, the president of the university (a liberal academic of international renown) was hemmed on the stage by two black-jacketed black students, one of them carrying a plank. Another black student took the microphone and said that that afternoon's seminar had decided that the president of the university (whom he referred to, deliberately humiliatingly, by his surname only) should be required to answer a question: would the university immediately get rid of its equity shares in the Chase National Bank, which apparently has branches in South Africa or something? The president, admirably maintaining dignity under impossible conditions, said that his difficulty in replying to that was that the university did not at present hold any shares in the Chase National Bank, because it had switched out of them for investment reasons some time ago. This reply was so clearly disappointing that one of the black-power-uniformed thugs seized him by the scruff of the neck and started to propel him off the stage. A band of black drummers beat an accompaniment to this.

At this stage the situation was partly saved by one of the nice black South African revolutionaries invited to our seminar who, with some courage, mounted the stage and said that, although he disapproved of the university murdering thousands of people by pouring all its investment money into white South Africa (which it is not doing), he nevertheless also disapproved of reasonable academics like the president being "more or less assaulted." It was proposed that another black man should give a speech introducing the congressman. This he did at such inordinate length that the meeting fortunately went to sleep.

Next day I lunched with this university president and his charming wife and small children. All doors to his office were locked, and we drove to his home accompanied by two security men. The talk over pre-lunch drinks was of another university president who had died of a heart attack during his university's latest "trouble," and of yet another who had just had the door of his house kicked down. Certainly, the dead president had had a weak heart already, and certainly the majority even of extremist students are mortified when such incidents occur; but that, not unnaturally, is not a great comfort to recall at such a lunch. It is filthy that America should tolerate that families of this decency and international eminence should have to live under these conditions of persisting apprehension; and, of course, America is not going to tolerate it for long. Certainly, it is even more filthy that millions of the great mass of decent black Americans of no international eminence should live under some of the same conditions of persisting apprehension. But—and this is the major reason why all honest liberals now need to unite in putting a term to violence—both groups are threatened by exactly the same thing.

The ghettos' Capones

For we come now to the much more serious effect of America's crazy encouragement of minority mob rule in recent years: the intimidation against the mass of Negroes themselves. An article in *The Observer* last January, with whose philosophy I wholly disagreed—it talked the usual 1966-style liberal stuff about the unlovable Mayor Daley of Chicago and other machine bosses going "all out to smash the war on poverty, with its intended aims of giving money and therefore power to programmes run by the poor themselves"—included the following story:

> A leading Negro journalist, assigned to write about a nationalist group, found himself giving a lift in his car to some of its members. Without asking him, they

93

loaded the boot with guns wrapped in blankets. The
significance is not just that he did not report or write
about the incident: it is that they were confident in
advance that he would not.

I asked Negroes I met whether this story was likely to
be true. The majority answer was "yes," and with two
points added. First, the reason why the average Negro
nowadays goes along with this sort of thing is not generally soul brotherhood. It is fear. In a public opinion
poll carried out for the Columbia Broadcasting System
last year, where anonymity was preserved, only 1 per
cent of Negroes said they would give active support to
Ron Karenga, 2 per cent to H. Rap Brown, 4 per cent
to Stokely Carmichael, while 49 per cent said they
would give it to the successor of Dr Martin Luther King.
  Secondly, the purpose of such guns hidden in car
boots would not always be to further the cause of Negro
revolution. It might be to rob banks. Under the increasingly bogus cover of political organisation—while
we liberal intellectuals insultingly tell one another that
the general anti-white mood among black Americans is
similar to the anti-German mood among the French in
1943—the Negro community is now breeding its Al
Capones. These are not the drama-seeking kids who get
photographed, who might be called the silly overground:
the real underground is far nastier even than the worst
of the overground makes itself look.
  It is not awfully surprising that a black American

94

agrees to be intimidated by this sort of horror of guns-in-the-boot. It sometimes seems as if the whole of America is now fearfully intent on passing violence by on the other side. The commonest individual philosophy seems to be that, so long as people are not being killed before one's eyes, one does not see why one should risk being uselessly killed oneself. To this is added the fact that public opinion polls show that a majority of Negroes have no confidence that the largely white police provide adequate protection in Negro areas: some because they think the police have allowed themselves to be overwhelmed, others because they think the police treat all Negroes as inferior beings anyway, others because they think the police are guilty of corrupt collusion with narcotics traffic and other lucrative ghetto crimes—most, probably, because they believe, almost certainly rightly, that each of these charges has some validity in at least some instances.

Those who are becoming the Al Capones in these grim urban jungles often want to keep the ghettos as they are: these are their constituencies. That is another reason why the most vital task before America today is to press forward with the break-up of the ghettos, and the suburbanisation of the Negro, at maximum pace. The means of furthering this advance becomes important. The particularist approach—working within Negro communities to improve the quality of labour that commutes from there—is going to become more and more difficult, because it has to be operated within communi-

95

ties that are themselves decaying. The generalist approach—such as by pushing forward with total economic expansion even at the risk of price inflation, and levelling up welfare assistance by a negative income tax—has become, I believe, steadily more desirable for the United States. To this, the last chapter turns.

The
Particular
and
the
General

How can America get out of its mess?

In the last few years the United States has pursued with extraordinary energy and resource a remarkable range of particularist policies to try to improve the quality and opportunities of its underclass. Programmes fall over one another at every street corner, often alas with a bang. Among the most prominent attempts and suggestions:

(1) Devoted efforts have been made under the Head Start programme to give pre-school training to children from the poorest homes. This is because all the social research and computers proved in the early 1960s that development of intelligence depends crucially on environment in the first five years of life. Unfortunately, despite an expenditure of over $1,000 per year per pupil for half-day sessions, all the social research and com-

puters in the late 1960s have shown, to quote President Nixon's recent report to Congress, that "the long-term effect of Head Start appears to be extremely weak." A Head-Start-follow-through programme is therefore under way.

(2) A whole range of public programmes and agencies exist to give special training and special help in job placement to the hard-core underemployed in the northern cities. As the most extravagant example, the residential training centres of the Job Corps were costing over $8,000 a year per enrollee in 1967. Mr Nixon is now closing the dearest of these down.

(3) As a very American device, under the Job Opportunities in the Business Sector (called JOBS) programme, leading business corporations are making real efforts to employ precisely the people whom their personnel departments have been scientifically trained to spot and reject for years. "Our preference for a vacancy nowadays," says one executive, "is a wild-eyed, kookily dressed, inept, bad timekeeping, illiterate young Negro with a minimum of three convictions for armed robbery or rape." This JOBS programme is being helped forward by government grants to meet the costs of training (average grant $3,000 per "disadvantaged" employee), but it sprang out of big corporations' fear of what is happening in riot-torn America today. "The president of General Motors," explains James Sundquist in that admirable *Agenda for the Nation*, "stood atop his building and saw Detroit in flames."

But the difficulty with JOBS is often that of getting the black worker from his home in the ghetto to certain, designated, participating factories in scattered suburban areas. To quote James Sundquist again:

> Typically, the poor lack reliable private transportation (they have broken-down jalopies or none at all, and many lack drivers' licences), and the circuitous public transportation routes may require two bucks and three hours, as one worker put it.

The Kerner commission suggested a system of generalised subsidies whereby the hard-core unemployed could be given green cards, and any employer anywhere who employed them could get a tax reduction. Obviously, such a system would be open to abuse, no doubt with some cards being sold; but this would be a generalised and free market system of subsidy, and I doubt if the present good-hearted system of planning to hire workers one does not want will long survive.

Little scope in the ghettos

(4) Some efforts have been made to persuade manufacturing firms to establish plants in the ghettos. Except in a few places—mostly roomier cities where the Negro areas are almost suburban—I do not believe that these efforts will work on any substantial scale. It is crazy

99

economics in a wide open country like America to try to direct factories into precisely those areas where the land is already most crowded with existing buildings, where environmental services are already appalling and overstrained, labour is unskilled, insurance and city tax rates exorbitantly high, and transport for products and materials has to pass through jammed streets to yards where pilfering is enormous. What might be possible is new commercial building in the ghettos.

New office blocks are still shooting up in other parts of Manhattan island, and it ought to be possible to shift some up a few streets to Harlem. In present conditions most of the office workers would no doubt commute from outside Harlem, and there would have to be a well-policed tunnel to the nearest subway station; but the money provided by the building could help those whose homes are displaced to move out of the ghetto—and this is greatly to be desired.

(5) Mr Nixon's campaign promises to foster "black capitalism" in the ghettos would run into the same difficulties as other ghetto enterprises, and some additional ones as well: existing black-owned businesses in the ghettos often carry on under a reign of terror from the depredations of protection gangs, hoodlums, and constant thefts. But it is worth noting the Kerner commission's reasoned argument that one of the Negro's great disadvantages, compared with earlier immigrants to the cities, is that small-time entrepreneurial opportunities have narrowed. Italian immigrants at the begin-

ning of the century set up shops in their areas largely to serve other incoming Italians who could not speak English, but the incoming Negroes do speak English and have arrived in cities teeming with shops already. There seems to me to be a case for opening up the Negroes' opportunity structure by some sort of special aid to small black capitalist ventures—but outside the ghettos, just as much as within them. Efforts are being made through the Small Business Administration to concentrate on this; they will need increasing support, because there is natural restiveness that $1 out of every $8 it has lent to minority groups has been lost.

(6) One supposed anti-poverty device in the United States is in fact a potent means of increasing poverty. This is the minimum wage of $1.60 an hour, enforced *101* by law throughout the country because the white-ruled trade unions like it; and because it seems natural to good-hearted people to say "how would you like to bring up a family on under $65 a week?" and "the average hourly wage is near to $3," and so on. The answer to them is that the way the system is imposed—and particularly the fact that it applies to young people's work—increases the number of those living in the poverty they abhor. All experience shows that when the rate is raised —and the Nixon administration has wisely refused to press forward with a Johnson administration scheme to increase it to $2—there is an increase in unemployment of Negro teenagers, part-time workers, and other marginal employees.

Employment is the key

This discussion of America's earnest efforts at particularist policies really does not suggest that the problems are going to be solved merely by mouthing more and more support for them. Certainly these earnest efforts should be continued, except for those that are actually increasing unemployment or giving more power to criminal groups. But my conclusion is that America's cause could best be served by taking four main economic decisions. None of them is likely to be popular with the Nixon administration.

102   The first important point is that America would be wise in the next decade to give almost an overstrained priority to maximum economic growth and the further expansion of full employment, even though this will mean tolerating more inflation than the middle classes will wish. One can see all the objections. It is easy to say that if one ran the economy for the next ten years at 4 per cent official unemployment instead of 3 per cent, and still aimed at 4 per cent annual growth from there, one should be able to keep price inflation to a tolerable 2 per cent per annum or so; and that the only macro-economic cost of thus bringing inflation down might be this once-for-all reduction of 1 per cent in capacity working—so that, e.g., the country would reach in December of 1980 the level of production that it

would otherwise reach in September of 1980. If America had no Negro problem, one would agree that this small price for curbing inflation would be infinitely well worth paying.

But America does have a Negro problem, and nice calculations of this kind therefore miss the whole nasty point. This nasty point is that any rise in unemployment is likely to hit disproportionately hard at militant Negro youth, who already (see page 83) have an underemployment rate far higher than the official unemployment figures suggest and whose numbers are due to rise by 40 per cent in the decade to the mid-1970s. The Kerner report last year defined the typical Negro rioter in 1967 as:

103

a teenager or young adult, a lifelong resident of the city in which he rioted, a high school drop-out—but somewhat better educated than his Negro neighbour— and almost invariably underemployed or employed in a menial job. He was proud of his race, extremely hostile to both whites and middle class Negroes, and, though informed about politics, highly distrustful of the political system and of political leaders.

The key points there are "somewhat better educated than his Negro neighbour" and "almost invariably underemployed or employed in a menial job." The first of these points gives the lie to the widespread white American belief that the black unemployed today are the unemployable. The second emphasises that even the great economic growth of the 1960s has managed to stop short at precisely the point where increased employment is most vital. Unfortunately, however, there is no denying that greater employment of this sub-class would be inflationary; no doubt they would be somewhat less efficient than the average of existing workers, so that marginal costs (and the bargaining power of existing workers) would rise.

If the objection to risking inflation to absorb these people is internal, then objectors should look at the alternatives. If the objection to inflation is its effect on the balance of payments, then America needs to press forward all the more urgently with the projects for greater international liquidity and for more freely floating exchange rates, in which the most progressive men of the Nixon administration in any case believe. It is not wise to say that a 1 per cent diminution in the annual rate of inflation is well worth purchasing at the cost of letting race war in America blaze.

Negative income tax

The second great economic and social need in the United States is the dispersion of population from the ghettos. A major requirement here is to get deserted welfare mothers and their large families out of the city centres, instead of ridiculously saying that they can draw higher benefits only if they stay there. The need is to nationalise the welfare system, replacing it by a negative income tax. It is probable that the Nixon administration will move what will be called part way towards this: by the federal government picking up more of the welfare bill (probably about $1½ billion worth a year), and insisting in return that all states must meet a certain minimum standard of outpayment. This will not suffice, because it will still leave welfare benefits in the liberal big northern cities more generous than in the conservative south.

The United States is proving to be fortunate that it is the only major industrial country that is not operating a system of children's allowances. This has allowed American economists, armed as usual with computers, to study dispassionately what would be the most efficient welfare system to have. More and more, expert opinion is agreeing that it would be some version of a negative income tax. Certainly the arguments one commonly hears in Britain—such as that negative or credit income taxes would have a greater disincentive effect than the existing British welfare system, or that it would be difficult to pay a negative income tax save at yearly intervals —are shown by American research to be off target.

Under the simplest proposal (by Earl Rolph and others) every man, woman, and child might be entitled to receive, say, $750 a year from the federal government —which, at least in some countries, could presumably be issued in weekly or monthly cheques or whatever—and would then have to pay a tax equal to one-third of income, not including the $750. The result is that any family with an income of under $2,250 a head would actually be getting a net sum from the government: over that figure it would be paying a net tax, but the marginal rate of tax would always be a third, so that there would be no addition of new disincentives. The basic method of payment can be varied in many ways, under proposals ranging from those of the conservative Milton Friedman (which might cost about $3 billion a year) to more ambitious schemes that would lift every American above the officially defined poverty line and help a lot of the near-poor besides (at a cost of about $25 billion a year).

It seems to me that it would be entirely possible—and immensely desirable—for America to move to one of these more ambitious schemes in the next five years. If President Nixon's team aims for rather over 4 per cent per annum real economic growth (risking some price inflation), and if it manages to close down the Vietnam war (which would probably save $20 billion a year, with a four-year lag before full effect), then the ordinary fiscal dividend should allow one of the $25 billion a year schemes to be brought into effect somewhere in the period between 1972 and 1974, even if Mr Nixon insists on retaining some tax money for more traditionally Republican priorities. Unfortunately, one difficulty is that a negative income tax scheme would have to be introduced over Arthur Burns's most strenuous protests.

Public workmen and open housing

Thirdly, there is something to be said for a modified version of the concept that was included rather vaguely in the Democratic platform for Hubert Humphrey's unsuccessful presidential attempt: namely, that the government should stand ready as the employer of last resort for those who could not get jobs in any other way. The argument here is that there are some 500,000 hard-core unemployed in the centres of cities; that creating 500,000 jobs would cost only about $2.5 billion a year; and that anybody who looks at the state of the streets and the general environment in the city centres, especially in the ghettos—at the public squalor amid private non-affluence—must realise that employing 500,000 more people to clean the places up, or to do domestic work in schools and perform some services as police auxiliaries, would be well worth while.

107

Those who advocate this should not underestimate the extent to which the removal of the hard-core unemployed would cause other costs and prices to creep up, especially in the service industries. Employers who are paying workmen at near to the minimum wage would have to increase their wages and prices if any of these government make-work jobs were at all attractive. And it is also worth insisting that a main objective of policy should be to help persuade people to move out of the ghettos, rather than keep them there doing the cleaning and other services that their own excessive presence makes necessary. That having been said, there is room for more public employment on environmental services in the cities—and it would be sensible for the federal government to pay for an extension of it.

The final need is to encourage exodus from the ghettos at all deliberate speed. One need here, already discussed, is the resolute enforcement of open housing laws—by taking infringements of the civil rights acts very speedily to court. Another device should be to give subsidies and tax credits to new industrial parks (like industrial estates in new towns in Britain) that are built well away from the centres of existing cities, and with approved housing schemes attached that must be racially mixed.

108

Decline and fall?

There is no point in pretending that I have great hopes that the policies recommended here will be remotely akin to those followed by any American government in the 1970s. Nothing that has been suggested in this survey is new, but almost every view in it is going rapidly out of fashion. The right wing of America's establishment will say that the expansionist argument gravely underestimates the evil that will be done to the United States if inflationary psychology is allowed to catch hold.

The left wing will say there is something beautiful in the fact that black Americans are now imbibing a dose of nationalism and pride in their own race and that the great need is to "keep up a conversation" with those who are being "driven to violence."

The reasons why the United States is proving so bad at handling its fairly normal historical crisis are rooted, I believe, in the fact that it has always been lucky enough to be a predominantly bourgeois-plus-yeoman society. Its right wing has never had reason to reflect, as we in Europe have done, that the awkward stage of history when an indigenous underclass has just been sucked by an industrial revolution into the mess and insecurity of urban society is a stage which it is crucial to dash through at maximum economic pace. America's urban underclass   *109* in years past has consisted of the most progressive types of immigrants, chasing upwards after the American dream, in conditions of natural boom which their own energetic arrival has helped to create. Meanwhile, America's left wing does not understand, as we in Europe most grimly learned in Germany and Italy between the wars, that violent nationalism is a heady drug that it is unsafe for an indignant and despairing urban lower middle class to see peddled among its young even in the smallest doses; and it is among the young lower middle class Negroes—not the pure underclass—that the most dangerous figures are now arising. This is another reason why the view of middle class white liberals, that we must hold a conversation with those "driven to violence," seems to me to be essentially lacking in compassion, because those who are really hurt by this are the humble souls who then have to live with violence as a neighbour.

Does this mean that anybody with my views should be desperately worried at the prospects ahead? At times in Washington in February, when apparently sober people told me of the rifles they kept at home "in case trouble comes," I did feel that the most appropriate texts for a reporter on America in 1969 might be found in the story of the decline and fall of another mighty empire that Gibbon started as he wandered round another Capitol. The pertinent, though scattered, phrases seem to abound.

110   *The decline of Rome was the natural and inevitable effect of immoderate greatness. Prosperity ripened the principle of decay. . . . The most potent and forcible cause of destruction, the domestic hostilities of the Romans themselves. . . . At such a time . . . when none could trust their lives or properties to the impotence of law, the powerful citizens were armed for safety, or offence, against the domestic enemies whom they feared or hated. . . . The nobles usurped the prerogative of fortifying their houses. . . . It was once proposed to discriminate the slaves by a peculiar habit; but it was justly apprehended that there might be some danger in acquainting them with their own numbers.*

They are acquainted with their own numbers in the

cities of America in 1969; the rallying symbol is black.

Even on cool reflection, I do not entirely dismiss these dangers. We have seen several times in the last year—for example, in France and Pakistan—the extraordinary pass to which riotous and even unarmed minorities of youth can bring a country. In the United States, where the cohorts of dissatisfied 16- to 25-year-old Negroes in the cities are due to increase so massively in the next few years, it is by no means certain that the rioters will be unarmed. Some time, I suspect, the guns may go blazing. And yet, even as one apprehends this, the point recurs that, according to all public opinion polls and all secret ballot elections, one is talking here about revolutionaries among a tiny minority within the minority of the black oppressed and the emotional young. *111* As the not exactly conservative, but nowadays rather likeable, Mr Mohammad Ali (*né* Cassius Clay) said to a bespectacled television interviewer: "For black people to start shooting in their fight against American society would be as silly as for you to get up and start hitting me."

And perhaps the final antidotes to despair are to go into America's heartland, behind the troubled coasts, where families still sleep at night with all the outside doors of their homes unlocked; or else, within the greatest urban jungle of all, to mount the Empire State building and look on that well-known skyline once again; or (although this sounds a strange place in which to soothe the nerves), to pause once more among the computers of Wall Street. For this after all—and probably in the end above all—is the society in which the last important stage of man's long economic revolution is succeeding. Somehow, in the farthest recesses of one's intellect, where presumably judgment lies, one doubts whether the United States is really liable to lose its foothold on this last, steep, thirty years' climb before the country reaches what all except the most neurotic of the status-afflicted should regard as material sufficiency for all its inhabitants.

112